SRI LANKA
in Pictures

Sara E. Hoffmann

Twenty-First Century Books

Contents

Twenty-First Century Books
A division of Lerner Publishing Group
241 First Avenue North
Minneapolis, MN 55401 U.S.A.

Website address: www.lernerbooks.com

web enhanced @ www.vgsbooks.com

Library of Congress Cataloging-in-Publication Data

Hoffmann, Sara E., 1978–
        Sri Lanka in pictures / by Sara E. Hoffmann.
          p.   cm. – (Visual geography series)
        Includes bibliographical references and index.
        ISBN-13: 978-0-8225-3481-5 (lib. bdg. : alk. paper)
        ISBN-10: 0-8225-3481-9 (lib. bdg. : alk. paper)
        1. Sri Lanka—Juvenile literature. 2. Sri Lanka—Pictorial works—Juvenile literature. I. Title. II. Visual
geography series (Minneapolis, Minn.)
DS489.H69 2006
954.93'0022'2—dc22   2005015639

Manufactured in the United States of America
1 2 3 4 5 6 – BP – 11 10 09 08 07 06

INTRODUCTION

On December 26, 2004, tremors from an earthquake on the floor of the Indian Ocean set off a tsunami (tidal wave) in southern Asia and eastern Africa. The tsunami slammed into the coasts of Sri Lanka, sweeping away entire villages and destroying schools, hospitals, and seaside hotels. The disaster took the lives of more than 30,000 Sri Lankans and left about 900,000 others without homes. In addition to the toll it took in lives and property, the tsunami also did substantial damage to Sri Lanka's economy. Instability continues as Sri Lanka works to restore its industries and to assist the hundreds of thousands displaced by the tsunami.

While the tsunami is the most devastating disaster to strike Sri Lanka, the nation is no stranger to hardship. Civil strife has plagued the country for more than twenty years. Sri Lanka's 19 million inhabitants come from many different ethnic groups, and these groups have often disagreed about how Sri Lanka should develop as a nation. Sri Lanka's population is primarily a mixture of Sinhalese (descendants of people from northern India) and Tamil (people whose roots lie in southern India). The island also is home to a large Muslim population, as well as people of European ancestry. After Sri Lanka achieved independence from Britain in 1948, disputes occurred between the Tamil minority and the Sinhalese majority. Because they see themselves at a political and cultural disadvantage in Sri Lanka, Tamil militants have sought to establish a separate Tamil state in Sri Lanka's northern and eastern provinces. The Sri Lankan government has refused to allow such a state to exist.

From this conflict, a Tamil guerrilla movement has emerged. The movement's members have engaged in terrorist activities, killing and injuring both civilians and government troops. In response, Sri Lankan soldiers have attacked Tamil villages. In the late 1980s, troops from India (whose own Tamil population supports the rebels) tried to help Sri Lanka persuade the Tamil guerillas to lay down their weapons. These efforts failed, however, and in the early 1990s,

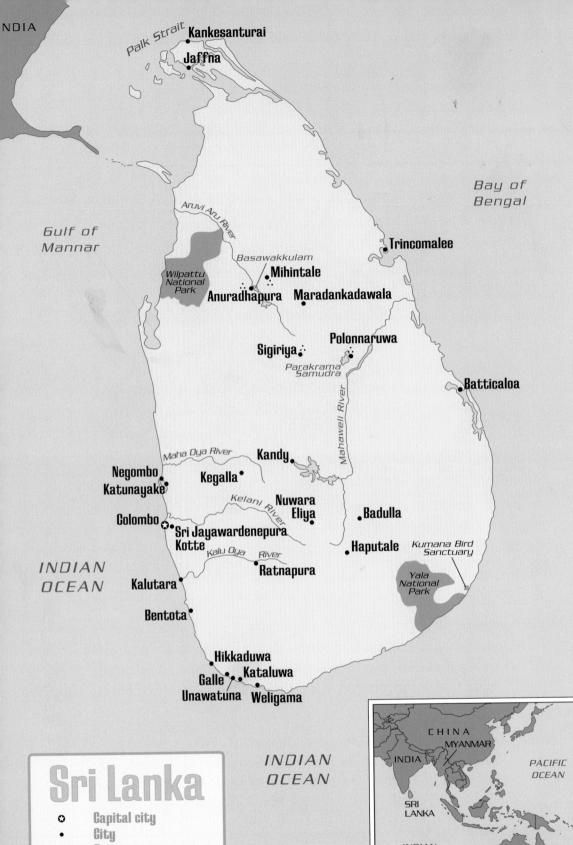

NDIA

Palk Strait

Kankesanturai

Jaffna

Gulf of Mannar

Aruvi Aru River

Bay of Bengal

Trincomalee

Basawakkulam

Mihintale

Wilpattu National Park

Anuradhapura   Maradankadawala

Sigiriya ∴   Polonnaruwa

Parakrama Samudra

Mahawell River

Batticaloa

Maha Oya River   Kandy

Negombo
Katunayake

Kegalla

Kelani River

Nuwara Eliya

Badulla

Colombo

Sri Jayawardenepura Kotte

Kalu Oya   *River*

Haputale

Kumana Bird Sanctuary

Ratnapura

Kalutara

Yala National Park

Bentota

INDIAN OCEAN

Hikkaduwa

Galle   Kataluwa

Unawatuna   Weligama

INDIAN OCEAN

Sri Lanka

☆ Capital city
• City
∴ Ruins

0   50 Miles
0   50 KM

N

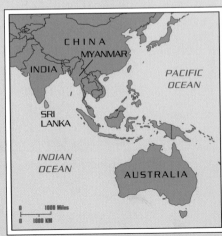

CHINA

MYANMAR

INDIA

PACIFIC OCEAN

SRI LANKA

INDIAN OCEAN

AUSTRALIA

0   1000 Miles
0   1000 KM

violence continued to claim Sri Lankan lives and to leave thousands of people homeless.

In 2002 the Sri Lankan government and the Tamil separatists formally agreed to a cease-fire. But negotiations stalled in the following year, and a 2004 suicide bombing in Sri Lanka's capital threatened to undo the shaky peace. The peace process sustained another apparent blow in 2005. In August of that year, Sri Lanka's foreign minister was assassinated. Shortly after the assassination, however, the Tamil separatists agreed to talk with the Sri Lankan government. But the government rejected the separatists' chosen location for the talks.

Sri Lanka's beauty belies its troubled history. Known as Ceylon until 1972, Sri Lanka is an island republic surrounded by the Indian Ocean. Sri Lanka is rich with beaches and has a tropical climate. Because of its location between the Middle East and Southeast Asia, the country has attracted traders, conquerors, and colonizers from all over the world. In spite of these international influences, a strong local culture has thrived, absorbing cultural elements from the Arabs, the Chinese, the Portuguese, the Dutch, and the British who came to the island.

THE LAND

Covering 25,332 square miles (65,610 square kilometers) in the Indian Ocean, the island of Sri Lanka lies just off the southeastern coast of India. The Gulf of Mannar and the Palk Strait run between Sri Lanka and the Indian subcontinent, but a chain of shoals (sandbanks) known as Adam's Bridge almost connects the island to its large northern neighbor. Sri Lanka's greatest length is 270 miles (435 km) from north to south, and its greatest width is 140 miles (225 km) from west to east. To the east of the island is the Bay of Bengal, which stretches from India to Myanmar. In area, Sri Lanka is slightly larger than the state of West Virginia and includes several small islands off its northern and northwestern coasts in its territory.

The 2004 tsunami damaged 80 percent of Sri Lanka's coasts, with the northern, eastern, and southern coasts bearing the brunt of the damage. The country's west coast and interior regions were mostly unaffected.

▶ Topography

Sri Lanka has two main landscape features. The Coastal Lowlands encircle the island, and a section of Central Highlands covers much of the southwestern and central part of the country. Stretching between 5 and 25 miles (8 and 40 km) inland from the coast are rolling plains that encompass the major portion of Sri Lanka's territory. Although the region is generally low and flat, occasional hills—actually underground masses of granite that have pushed through the earth—break up the landscape. The soil in the region is made up of loose stone and eroded rock, except for the northern Jaffna Peninsula, which consists of limestone.

The plains gradually rise in elevation in south central Sri Lanka to form the Central Highlands, which vary in height from 3,000 feet (914 meters) to more than 8,000 feet (2,438 m). Narrow ravines, deep valleys, and high plateaus interrupt the highland landscape, which covers the remaining one-fifth of Sri Lanka's territory.

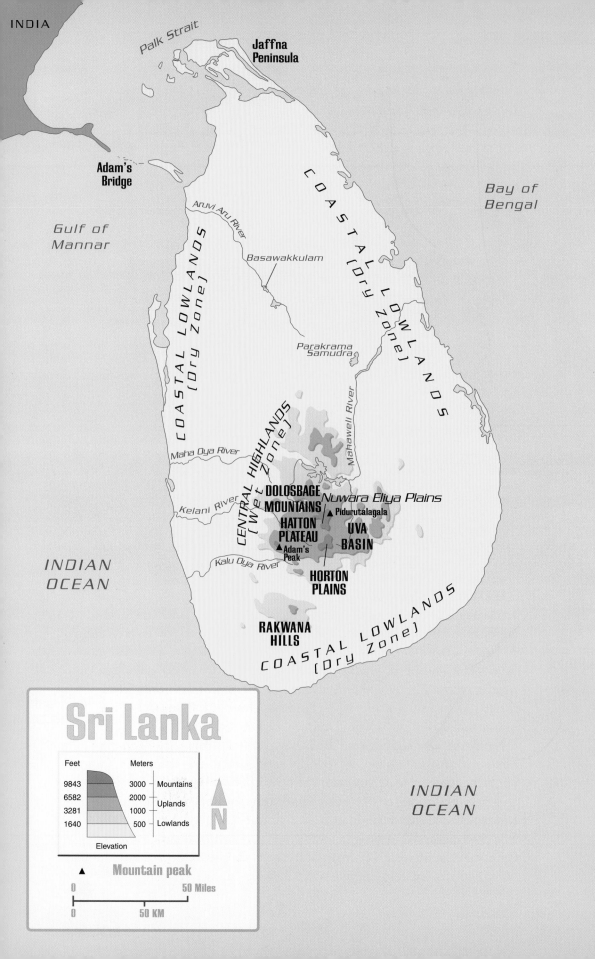

INDIA

Palk Strait

Jaffna
Peninsula

COASTAL LOWLANDS (Dry Zone)

Bay of
Bengal

Adam's
Bridge

Aruvi Aru River

Basawakkulam

Gulf of
Mannar

COASTAL LOWLANDS (Dry Zone)

*Parakrama
Samudra*

Mahaweli River

Maha Oya River

Kelani River

**DOLOSBAGE
MOUNTAINS** *Nuwara Eliya Plains*

▲ *Pidurutalagala*

CENTRAL HIGHLANDS (Wet Zone)

**HATTON
PLATEAU**

**UVA
BASIN**

▲ *Adam's
Peak*

INDIAN
OCEAN

Kalu Oya River

**HORTON
PLAINS**

**RAKWANA
HILLS**

*COASTAL LOWLANDS
(Dry Zone)*

Sri Lanka

Feet	Meters	
9843	3000	Mountains
6582	2000	Uplands
3281	1000	
1640	500	Lowlands

Elevation

▲ Mountain peak

N

0	50 Miles

0	50 KM

INDIAN
OCEAN

A long, central ridge within the highlands features Pidurutalagala, the nation's highest peak at 8,281 feet (2,524 m) above sea level. Nearby are the high, fertile plains of Nuwara Eliya and Horton, where tea plants thrive. Plateaus, such as the Hatton Plateau to the west and the Uva Basin to the east, flank the central ridge. The western plateau contains Adam's Peak (7,360 ft. or 2,243 m), which for centuries has been a place of religious pilgrimage for people of the Islamic, Hindu, Buddhist, and Christian faiths. Other uplands, including the Rakwana Hills and the Dolosbage Mountains, lie south and north-west of the central ridge.

Climate

Because of its location near the equator, Sri Lanka's climate is primarily warm and tropical. On most parts of the island, temperatures remain between 60°F (15°C) and 90°F (32°C) throughout the year. However, there are climate variations in Sri Lanka. Sea breezes moderate lowland temperatures, and high altitudes cool the mountainous areas. The coastal city of Colombo averages 77°F (25°C) in January and 82°F (28°C) in May, while mountainous Nuwara Eliya records temperatures of 57°F (14°C) and 60°F (15°C) in the same two months.

Sri Lanka's Coastal Lowlands and Central Highlands can be characterized by their differing amounts of seasonal rainfall. Therefore, the Coastal Lowlands and inland areas—with their relatively low precipitation levels—are called the Dry Zone, and the moist highlands are known as the Wet Zone. The Dry Zone extends over four-fifths of the island's territory. This zone contains most of the coastal belt, which rises from sea level to 100 feet (30 m) and is 25 miles (40 km) across at its widest point.

ADAM'S PEAK

Adam's Peak, a tall mountain in southwestern Sri Lanka, features a footprintlike formation at its summit. People of many different faiths make pilgrimages to Adam's Peak to see the "footprint." Muslims believe that the print belongs to Adam, an important figure in the Islamic, Jewish, and Christian religions. Hindus attribute the mark to Shiva, one of the gods in the Hindu faith. Buddhists, meanwhile, claim that the indentation is from Gautama Buddha, the Indian philosopher who founded Buddhism.

Although Adam's Peak is a sacred site for many, the mountain is also a favorite destination for those who enjoy nature. The summit affords a beautiful view of Sri Lanka's hill country—especially at sunrise.

The Wet Zone in the southwestern part of Sri Lanka benefits from the southwest monsoon, a seasonal wind that occurs between May and November. It carries heavy rainfall—sometimes as much as 200 inches (508 centimeters). Precipitation levels in the Wet Zone usually average more than 100 inches (254 cm) per year, however.

The Dry Zone in the northeastern region receives the northeast monsoon. It arrives from the Bay of Bengal between December and February. Annual rainfall in the Dry Zone is between 50 inches (127 cm) and 75 inches (190 cm), and most crops in the northern and eastern lowlands require irrigation. Two relatively arid zones along the southeastern and northwestern coasts get between 25 inches (63 cm) and 50 inches (127 cm) of rainfall each year.

Drought and flooding are common problems in Sri Lanka, due to deforestation and land erosion. During the two periods between the monsoons, thunderstorms are more frequent in the Wet Zone than in the Dry Zone.

◎ Rivers and Lakes

Most of Sri Lanka's rivers begin in the Central Highlands and travel over steep waterfalls before flowing through the inland plains to the Indian Ocean. Of the nation's sixteen major waterways, the Mahaweli

This red sunset in Unawatuna, Sri Lanka, looks stormy. Monsoon winds bring heavy rains to Sri Lanka's Dry Zone as well as to its Wet Zone.

This **elephant herd bathing in the Maha Oya River** is from the Pinnawela Elephant Orphanage near Kegalla, Sri Lanka.

River is the longest and flows for 206 miles (332 km) through the Dry Zone to Trincomalee on the northeastern coast. In the 1980s, the government completed a project to develop the Mahaweli as a source of hydroelectric power and irrigation for the Dry Zone. The Kelani River ends near Colombo, the capital city, on the western coast. The Kalu Oya reaches the Indian Ocean near Kalutara on the southwestern coast, and the Aruvi Aru flows northwestward across the Dry Zone to the Gulf of Mannar.

The rivers effectively irrigate and drain the highlands because the waterways flow swiftly downward to their sea outlets. In contrast, on the plain and along the coast—where the terrain is level—water sometimes collects and floods settlements, roads, and farmland. As a result, homes and overland routes in these regions usually lie far from the riverbanks.

Although Sri Lanka contains few lakes, it does have a number of artificial reservoirs known as tanks, some of which are more than two thousand years old. The oldest of these tanks is Basawakkulam, which was constructed in 300 B.C. It was built to collect and store water for the ancient city of Anuradhapura in north central Sri Lanka.

Flora and Fauna

The vegetation of Sri Lanka reflects the island's climate pattern and topography. Thus the well-watered regions of the Central Highlands and of the southwestern coast are lush with vegetation, and evergreen rainforests are common. Hundreds of species of flowering shrubs—including hibiscus, frangipani, bougainvillea, tree ferns, and orchids—are found along with groves of mango, cinnamon, cacao, and banana trees. Rubber plantations lie between the highland tea estates and the coastal coconut plantations.

Cinnamon is made of the dried inner bark of **cinnamon tree stems and twigs** that are less than 2 inches (5 cm) in diameter. On a small islet near Hikkaduwa, a worker carefully scrapes and collects this inner bark. Sri Lanka produces more than 80 percent of the cinnamon consumed annually around the world.

In Sri Lanka and on other islands in the Pacific Ocean, **pandanus trees** grow up to 30 feet (9 m) in height and to 35 feet (11 m) in diameter. A pandanus tree develops support or prop roots at its base and sometimes along its branches. These roots loop upward from the ground, making the tree look like it is standing on its tiptoes. Go to www.vgsbooks.com for links to more infomation about the land, plants, and animals of Sri Lanka.

In addition to forests and thick jungles, the elevated plateaus have limited areas of coarse grass, called *patanas*. The wet patanas cover the Horton Plains and the area around Nuwara Eliya, and the dry patanas grow especially well in the Uva Basin.

In the Coastal Lowlands, many varieties of palm trees—including areca and coconut—thrive. Mangroves and pandanus trees grow well in coastal areas. Trees used for lumber, such as mahogany, are native to the Wet Zone, and acacias, eucalypti, and cypresses also grow in various parts of the region.

In the Dry Zone, fertile soil and long-established systems of irrigation keep the countryside green. Much of the Dry Zone has scrub vegetation and forests that include ebony, satinwood, and many other valuable trees. The eastern region features a few grassland areas, called *talawas*. In these regions, however, desert conditions can arise if monsoon rains fail to appear.

A Sixth Sense?

While the tsunami ravaged Sri Lanka's coastlines and killed and injured many people, few animals have been reported dead. Some people have speculated that the animals sensed the impending tsunami and sought shelter before it occurred. People who were at Yala National Park on December 26, 2004, claim that they saw elephants running to higher ground just before the waves hit.

Some scientists believe that animals can detect the atmospheric changes that take place before an event such as a storm. For example, an animal may sense a shift in barometric pressure or feel the pre-tremors of an earthquake. Yet other scientists disagree and believe that no conclusive evidence links animals' behavior to natural occurrences.

Sri Lanka is famous for the variety of its wild animals, which are protected by law. Along with elephants, larger animals include bears, wild boars, leopards, cheetahs, deer, and buffalo. Reserves such as Wilpattu and Yala national parks preserve the natural habitats of these animals. Although Yala was damaged in the 2004 tsunami, it remains one of the best places in Sri Lanka for observing wildlife.

A sanctuary at Kumana on the southeastern coast protects birds from hunters and animal predators. Peacocks are native to the island, as are many other remarkable species of birdlife.

The sea around Sri Lanka's southern coral reef is home to many beautiful fish, including sturgeons, Moorish idols, and butterfly fish. However, pollution threatens to harm the fish and other marine species. Months after the tsunami struck, debris still littered the waters off Sri Lanka's southern coast. Scientists advised a cleanup effort to protect the reefs and other ocean life.

Natural Resources and Environmental Concerns

Precious stones are the most renowned of Sri Lanka's mineral resources. More than 90 percent of the island's gems come from a relatively small area near the southwestern city of Ratnapura, whose name means "city of gems." Gems appear at the base of the Central Highlands, where mountain streams have left deposits of gravel. Sri Lanka's gems include diamonds, rubies, sapphires, moonstones, garnets, amethysts, topazes, cat's-eyes, aquamarines, and emeralds. Sri Lanka has become one of the world's leading producers of graphite, a material with many industrial uses. Some other minerals found in Sri Lanka are iron ore, monazite, and uranium.

Extensive mining in Sri Lanka has resulted in degradation of the country's coastlines and coral reefs. In addition to land-based mining, many people mine the reefs, as coral is used to make concrete. Pollution, made worse by tourism, further degrades the coastlines. Builders clear mangrove swamps and other ecosystems to make way for resorts and hotels. Soil erosion and deforestation (the practice of clearing forests for building and development) are grave threats to the island's natural environment. Wild animals such as cheetahs, leopards, and monkeys are casualties of increased industrialization and population growth.

Tourists sometimes destroy Sri Lanka's coral reefs. They break off bits of coral for souvenirs. Another threat to the coral reefs comes from boaters. When boaters drop anchors into the water, they sometimes hit reefs and damage them.

Poaching (illegal killing) of wild animals is another serious environmental issue. Although Sri Lanka has laws in place to protect its wildlife, people still poach animals—particularly elephants, whose tendency to destroy farm crops can cost rural families significant portions of their annual incomes. Furthermore, because male elephants are prone to aggressive behavior, some people see poaching as an act of self-defense.

In order for elephants and other wildlife to survive outside of protected zones, people must recognize wild animals as an economic and cultural asset. Sri Lanka's wide variety of wildlife draws tourist dollars to the country. Many vacationers travel to the island to see its native plants and animals. The elephant is also a vital part of Sri Lankan culture. Elephant keepers called mahouts care for and create lasting bonds with the animals, and elephants play an important role in Sri Lanka's sacred religious festivals and processions.

Cities

Sri Lanka's urban areas are scattered around the country. However, almost every major settlement is connected to the others by road or rail. Colombo, Sri Lanka's commercial capital, is a bustling city with about 653,000 residents. Colombo was the capital of the Portuguese, Dutch, and British colonial administrations in Sri Lanka. Sri Lanka's legislative capital is Sri Jayawardenepura Kotte.

COLOMBO has a fine blend of architectural styles. Most of the buildings remain from British colonial times, when streets were widened and parks were created. Standing near temples and the city's mosques (Islamic places of worship) are colorful markets, such as the Pettah, which offer a wide variety of goods.

In 1878 the British dredged the bottom of the city's harbor and built protective seawalls. These improvements greatly expanded the port's capacity and eventually made Colombo's harbor the major trading center in Sri Lanka. The capital's international airport is also a travel hub of southern Asia and serves as a refueling station for major airlines.

JAFFNA Located at the northern peninsular tip of Sri Lanka, Jaffna is a seaport with a population of about 149,000. Although it lies in the driest part of Sri Lanka, Jaffna has an active trade in the tobacco, cotton, timber, and fruit industries. It is also a stronghold of Tamil nationalism (devotion and loyalty to the Tamil culture and interests).

Colombo's Galle Face Green is a busy public park along the Indian Ocean.

KANDY In the Central Highlands of Sri Lanka lies the city of Kandy, home to approximately 112,000 people. Once the capital of a powerful Sinhalese kingdom, Kandy has developed into the spiritual and cultural center of the nation. In Kandy, for example, Buddhists hold an important annual religious procession, or *perahera*, and Buddhist temples and historic sites abound.

GALLE, a port on the southern coast, has a population of about 94,000. This city was known to ancient Phoenician, Greek, and Roman traders. Its location on the sea route between the markets of the Middle East and south central Asia made Galle an important port until the nineteenth century, when the British developed Colombo as their main trading center.

TRINCOMALEE The more rugged northeastern coast contains Trincomalee, with an estimated population of 50,000. One of the best natural harbors in the world, this port's location was very important to the British during their rule of India and during World War II (1939–1945). Trincomalee handles export trade in tea, rubber, and coconuts and has many fine examples of religious temples and colonial architecture.

The 2004 tsunami badly damaged many of Sri Lanka's coastal cities. The coasts hardest hit were those populated with resorts and hotels. In areas untouched by development, natural formations such as sand dunes and coral reefs helped to absorb the impact of the rushing water.

HISTORY AND GOVERNMENT

According to an ancient text known as the *Mahavamsa* (written in the sixth century A.D.), the Sinhalese arrived in present-day Sri Lanka from mainland India in about 500 B.C. At the head of the landing party was Vijaya, an exiled Indian prince. Vijaya established a kingdom by conquering the inhabitants of the island, from whom the Wanniyala-aetto (Sri Lanka's indigenous people) descended.

The newcomers, originally a northern Indian people, spoke an Indo-European language closely related to Sanskrit and more distantly related to most of the languages of Europe, including English. (The modern Sinhala language is a direct descendant of this ancient speech.)

Vijaya encouraged people from mainland India to settle on the island, and he called his realm Sinhala, after his family name. His successors ruled a region located to the north of the Central Highlands. Among its other achievements, the Sinhala dynasty (family of rulers) engineered an elaborate irrigation system and constructed reservoirs to store water for crops.

The Arrival of Buddhism and the Tamil

In the third century B.C., during the reign of the Sinhalese king Devanampiya Tissa, the son of the Indian emperor Asoka traveled to Sri Lanka and introduced Buddhism to the island. After Devanampiya Tissa adopted Buddhism, the religious philosophy became an inseparable element of Sinhalese culture and inspired a rich and enduring artistic tradition throughout the country. The new faith unified the Sinhalese under their king, and as Buddhism disappeared in India, the Sinhalese saw themselves as the protectors of the Buddhist faith.

At roughly the same time, new arrivals—known as the Tamil—came to Sri Lanka from southern India. The Tamil spoke a Dravidian language, which was unlike any other in the region. They followed the Hindu religion, a faith with several important gods that conflicted with the strict Buddhism of the Sinhalese.

When groups of the Tamil began to settle in the northern part of Sri Lanka, the Sinhalese kings tried to stop them from establishing a community on the island. Battles between the two groups—who had sharp cultural and ethnic differences—continued for centuries. Nevertheless, the Tamil succeeded in settling northern Sri Lanka.

The Sinhala Dynasty

The country prospered under the ninety successive kings of the Sinhala dynasty, which lasted for more than 1,500 years. Art and science flourished, and a splendid capital city was laid out at Anuradhapura in the north central part of the island.

King Devanampiya Tissa built the first stupa—a memorial to Buddha in the form of a dome-topped mound—at Anuradhapura. Other Buddhist

STUPAS

Stupas are one of the most notable structures in Buddhist architecture. These dome-shaped shrines mark sites that are sacred to Buddhists. Stupas contain relics, or ancient artifacts, of Buddha. Historians have studied the relics found in ancient stupas to learn more about early Sinhalese society. Because many stupas are in ruins or have undergone renovations, it is difficult to know what ancient stupas may have looked like.

This small stupa is located in Mihintale near Anuradhapura.

This **early Sinhalese reservoir** in Sri Lanka still holds water. To learn more about Sri Lanka's history, go to www.vgsbooks.com for links.

monuments also dot the landscape, revealing the immense skill and ingenuity of early Sinhalese engineers. A vast network of reservoirs brought water into Anuradhapura, a sewer system removed waste, and stone swimming pools provided leisure and relaxation.

Sinhalese kings held complete power but, as Buddhists, had to obey strict rules regarding justice and equal treatment of their subjects. Buddhist monasteries flourished and produced fine literary and historical works, including the *Mahavamsa*. In addition, monastic elders, who organized into councils called *sanghas*, advised Sinhalese kings on matters of national importance.

Noble-born Sinhalese owned most of the farmland, and workers were attached by law to the land they farmed and owed loyalty and obedience to the landowner. The king's access to this free labor force was an important element in the progress of royal public works.

The vast irrigation system of tanks, canals, and sluices (water passageways) became the lifeline of the kingdom. Without the system, entire agricultural estates would return to their original dry condition. As a result, Sinhalese kings worked hard to maintain peace within the realm, for conflict could easily ruin the kingdom's delicate water supply lines.

Trade with Other Lands

Because of the island's location and fertile soil, the Sinhalese kingdom attracted many visitors. They included travelers from Rome, a large empire based in Italy. In the first century A.D., the Roman historian and geographer Pliny described the arrival in Rome of trade ambassadors from the Sinhalese kingdom. Not long after this early contact, direct trade between Sri Lanka and the Roman Empire began.

When the power of Rome declined in the fifth century, the exchange of the island's goods with Europe became indirect, falling largely into the hands of merchants and traders from the Arabian Peninsula. In the coming centuries, Arab traders—who called the island Serendib, an Arabic version of the Indian name Sinhala Dvipa—gained control of the western trade routes to Asia.

Meanwhile, Chinese traders began to develop ties to the kingdom. In the year 411, the Chinese explorer Fahsien arrived and wrote a detailed account of his visit. As a result, commercial relations developed between Sri Lanka and China. Direct trade with China ended after Malays—a people from the Malay Peninsula in Southeast Asia—took over the sea-lanes to Asia in the ninth century. Nevertheless, Sinhalese ports continued to be major trading depots, and by the tenth century, Galle was among the busiest ports in Asia.

The Rise of Polonnaruwa

Under the Sinhalese kingdom, the island was divided into three principal territories—Rajarata (with Anuradhapura as the capital), Ruhuna, and Malaya. Tamil kingdoms existed in India, as well as on Sri Lanka. Sinhalese kings used the rivalry among the Indian Tamil to maintain their own security by allying with one Indian Tamil kingdom to avoid being attacked by another.

In turn, the Tamil kingdoms in southern India hoped to expand their holdings by conquering the island. The Cholas, a Tamil people of southern India, put together one such expansionist policy.

In 1017 the Cholas captured the Sinhalese king Mahinda V and took him to India, where he died in 1029. Chola invaders destroyed Anuradhapura and ruled from Polonnaruwa, their capital. The new north central location allowed the Cholas to control overland routes to the southern territory of Ruhuna. Meanwhile, Buddhism took second place to the Hindu religion of the Tamil conquerors.

Resistance to Chola domination centered on Ruhuna, and in 1070 Vijayabahu I, a Sinhalese prince, overthrew the Cholas and regained

One of the oldest monuments in Polonnaruwa is the Vatadage. It was a circular structure with a diameter of 59 feet (18 m), built in the twelfth century.

control of Anuradhapura. He retained Polonnaruwa as the kingdom's capital, thereby securing Sinhalese predominance in the southern and central regions of the country.

The Reign of Parakramabahu I and Its Aftermath

Civil wars followed Vijayabahu's reign, when rivals to the throne competed with one another for supremacy. Eventually, Parakramabahu I took control of Polonnaruwa, unifying Sri Lanka under his rule, which began in 1153. Parakramabahu reorganized the government, raised the standard of living of the people, and carried out extensive public works. He built many tanks and canals, including the massive Parakrama Samudra (Sea of Parakrama), as well as several religious monuments.

Under Parakramabahu's influence, the Sinhalese kingdom became a major power in southern Asia. Seeking to expand his realm, the king launched an invasion of Myanmar (to the northeast) in about 1165. A few years later, he attacked the southern Indian kingdom of Pandya. In addition, the Sinhalese continued to launch campaigns against the Cholas.

This display of energy, however, also had some negative effects. Sinhalese invasions into foreign territory brought few lasting benefits, and the extensive building schemes relied upon enormous amounts of peasant labor and government revenue. Moreover, the dynamic personality of the king—rather than a strong political and economic base—became central to the success of the realm.

When Parakramabahu died in 1186, the Sinhalese kingdom declined almost immediately. Would-be successors fought one another for control, while foreign invaders chased the royal leaders and their people farther and farther south.

A Malay invasion in the thirteenth century caused Polonnaruwa—and its extensive irrigation works—to be abandoned. With the means of agricultural prosperity disrupted, the Sinhalese kingdom divided into small realms, each with its own main city. This move encouraged other groups, such as the Tamil, to exert their power.

LIKE FATHER, LIKE SON

In the fifteenth century, European monarchs raced to find the shortest, fastest, and safest trade route to the Indian subcontinent. King João II of Portugal commissioned Estavao da Gama to identify an all-water route to India. Estavao died before he could set sail, and his son Vasco took over, successfully reaching Calicut, India, in 1498. By then João II had also died. His successor Manuel I sent Francisco de Almeida to Calicut to become its first Portuguese viceroy (governor). In the same year, Almeida's son Lorenço was at sea south of India when monsoon winds forced his ship to take shelter at Galle, Sri Lanka, making him the first European to visit the island.

By the fourteenth century, southern Indian rulers had set up a Tamil kingdom on the northern Jaffna Peninsula. In the fifteenth century, Chinese forces controlled the island and Sinhalese kings paid money and handed over goods to agents of the Chinese Empire. When Europeans arrived in the early sixteenth century, a Sinhalese leader ruled from Kotte near present-day Colombo, and another held power in Kandy.

◉ The Arrival of the Portuguese

In 1505 Portuguese navigators visited Sri Lanka, docking near Colombo to find cinnamon and other spices. Within a few years, the Portuguese virtually controlled most of the coastal regions of the island, although they did not assume formal rule until 1597.

The Portuguese attempted to conquer the Sri Lankan interior, where profitable spice plants grew in abundance. But they met resistance from the mountain kingdom of Kandy. The Kandyans withstood Portuguese efforts to absorb them, and the Portuguese settled for acquiring only coastal areas of Sri Lanka, which they collectively called Cilao (a variation of the Arabic name Serendib).

Portugal's period of control brought several major changes to the island. The Portuguese introduced Christianity in the form of Roman Catholicism, brought in European styles of education, and developed the port of Colombo into a major trading center.

Spices have long been an important part of Sri Lankan culture. Sri Lanka's cuisine includes spices such as cinnamon, nutmeg, and cardamom (an aromatic, peppery condiment). Sri Lankan markets also sell spices for medicinal purposes. Traditional healers use spices to cure ailments such as fevers and coughs.

The Portuguese cemented anticolonial feeling among the Sinhalese by following a policy of intolerance toward other religions. They destroyed Hindu and Buddhist temples and persecuted Muslim traders who lived along the coast. Resistance to Portuguese rule centered on the still-independent Sinhalese kingdom of Kandy.

The Dutch Takeover and British Influence

In 1638 the Netherlands—a rival European trading power—drove out the Portuguese by making an alliance with the Kandyan kingdom. In exchange for a share of the cinnamon lands in Kandy, the Dutch agreed to take the island's port cities from the Portuguese and to return them to the Sinhalese. In this way, the Sinhalese recaptured Trincomalee and Batticaloa, but the Dutch retained the ports of Galle and Negombo and began to collect revenue from them. In time, the Dutch also tried to subdue Kandy but, like the Portuguese, failed.

Unable to control all the profitable cinnamon lands, the Dutch began to cultivate the spice in the lowlands. They also grew plantation crops, including coffee, coconuts, sugarcane, cotton, and tobacco. The most important Dutch legacy, however, was the introduction of Roman-Dutch laws that covered property and inheritance rights.

In the seventeenth and eighteenth centuries, another strong European power—Great Britain—also became active in the Indian Ocean. Through the British East India Company (a trading agency chartered by the British government), Britain gained control over the Indian subcontinent. In addition, Britain wanted a militarily safe, all-weather port to protect its holdings in eastern India. The Dutch agreed to allow the British to use Trincomalee as a naval base.

Relations between the Dutch and the British deteriorated in the late eighteenth century, and the Dutch withdrew permission to use Trincomalee. The British captured the port in 1796, effectively ending Dutch power on the island. Thereafter, Britain—first through its delegates in India and later directly—administered the island.

Initially, the British held only the coastal areas, as the two previous European powers had. The Kandyan kingdom remained independent. To consolidate their island holdings, the British declared their lands in Sri Lanka to be a colony in 1802. The British called their holdings Ceylon, after the Portuguese Ceilao. Meanwhile, internal disagreements in Kandy weakened the kingdom, making way for British campaigns against the highland realm.

The Nineteenth Century

Conflicts between the Sinhalese king Sri Wickrama Rajasinghe and his nobles helped the British to take over Kandy. Kandyan rebels invited the British to intervene in the dispute, and the royal Kandyan troops laid down their weapons without actually fighting Britain's forces. The British captured the king and sent him to southern India in 1815. The British and Sinhalese signed a treaty that formally ended hostilities.

Anticolonial rebellions flared in the next three years, however, among both Buddhist clergy and Sinhalese nobles, who felt edged out

Sri Wickrama Rajasinghe had this ornate retaining wall built around the artificial lake at the Temple of the Tooth in Kandy, Sri Lanka.

of power. In 1818 the British stopped using local Sri Lankan administrations to govern and later divided Kandy among surrounding provinces.

Large-scale agricultural development emerged in Ceylon during the nineteenth century. At first, the British raised coffee on their major estates, but low market prices and disease caused the British to replace this product with tea. Rubber and coconuts also found a steady market value and became important export crops. The plantation system required a large labor force—larger than the island's population could provide. As a result, the British began to encourage Tamil emigration from southern India.

In addition to developing an export economy, the British established road and rail connections to aid plantation owners. The British

In this photo from the late 1800s, tea plantation workers in Ceylon come in from the fields to weigh the tea leaves they have picked. The British hired many Tamil in India to work on British plantations in Ceylon.

Crews of hundreds of **Ceylonese workers built the island's railways** during the nineteenth century under British rule.

educational system—another important colonial innovation—began to change new generations of Sinhalese and Tamil. It prepared them for posts in the Ceylon Civil Service. Because they saw advantages in cooperating with the British, the Tamil held numerous posts at all levels of the colonial administration.

◉ Reform Movements

After more than seventy-five years of British rule, reform movements among local peoples—especially Buddhist monks and Ceylonese professionals—began to emerge. The Jaffna Association, the Ceylon National Association, and other groups pushed for changes in policy that would allow them more political power. In addition, a Buddhist movement encouraged people to return Buddhism to its dominant role in island society. Both monks and professionals ultimately desired independence. The professionals wanted to gain a more active role in the colonial government. The Buddhists sought to eliminate European influence and to strengthen Buddhism's status in the country.

The British tried to ease the conflicts by making minor policy changes, but the effort failed to calm the activists' concerns. Nationalists organized a railway strike in 1912, and the event stirred anticolonial sentiments among the colony's writers and poets. In 1915, after a religious disturbance occurred between Buddhists and Muslims, the British declared martial law (rule by the military) on the island. Harsh measures, including arbitrary arrests and killings, formed nationalist feelings into a driving force. As a consequence, the Ceylon National Congress, a group whose aim was to secure self-government for Ceylon, was established in 1919.

From Britain's point of view, the question was how to retain control of Ceylon's commerce, industry, and ports while giving the Ceylonese limited self-government. The British decided to write a constitution that would include more representation for local peoples. British control would remain in force through the document's newly formed States Council.

The Road to Independence

Many people were still pushing for an independent Ceylon when World War II spread to Southeast Asia. In 1942 the British lost their port at Singapore to the Japanese, and as a result, Trincomalee regained its position as a strategic outpost. The British recognized that a loyal colonial population would help them to win the war in the region. They promised self-government to the Ceylonese after global hostilities were over in order to gain the cooperation of the islanders during the war.

British navy admiral Lord Louis Mountbatten *(in white with hands clasped behind his back)* **addresses U.S. sailors** aboard the USS *Saratoga*, docked at Trincomalee, Ceylon, during World War II.

In 1946 the postwar British government in London approved the first Ceylonese constitution. The document had come about largely through the efforts of D. S. Senanayake, the colonial administration's minister of agriculture. In 1947, following widespread strikes, the British granted Ceylon commonwealth status, meaning that the former colony was self-governing but still associated with Great Britain. A majority of voters supported Senanayake's United National Party (UNP)—a coalition of the Ceylon National Congress, the Sinhala Maha Sabha Party, and the Muslim League. On February 4, 1948, Ceylon became a fully independent nation with Senanayake as its first prime minister.

Early Administrations

The UNP held power for eight years, beginning in 1948. D. S. Senanayake encouraged private enterprise and organized programs to raise the standard of living for Ceylonese citizens. Irrigation and hydroelectrical power plants brought needed agricultural improvements to the Dry Zone. The government built more schools, provided free education, and brought dangerous diseases, such as malaria, under control.

D. S. Senanayake died in a horse-riding accident in 1952, and his death destabilized the UNP. Senanayake's son Dudley, who had been educated in Britain, led the government for a brief period. One of Dudley Senanayake's first policies as prime minister was to provide free rice to every citizen in Sri Lanka. But rice prices soon began to rise around the world. As a result, Senanayake raised the price of rice in Sri Lanka—an extremely unpopular decision that led to mass rioting. Senanayake was forced to resign in 1953. His cousin, the equally Europeanized Sir John Kotelawala, followed him in office.

Buddhist nationalism—a force that independence had not really calmed—continued to grow, however. Conservative Buddhists wanted Ceylon to return to its Sinhalese Buddhist origins, under which the clergy had great authority within the political structure. Giving direction to this movement was a European-educated Sinhalese—S. W. R. D. Bandaranaike, leader of the Sinhala Maha Sabha. In 1951 he had left the UNP and renamed his wing of the organization the Sri Lanka Freedom Party (SLFP), which won the general elections of 1956.

Bandaranaike's government introduced Socialist reforms, including the nationalization (change from private to government ownership) of plantations and banks. Bandaranaike also chose to establish Sinhala as the country's official language—a move that underscored the nation's independence from its colonial past and the dominance of the Sinhalese majority.

The Tamil reacted strongly to this move, considering it a ploy to decrease their political influence and opportunities. Eventually, Bandaranaike agreed to make Tamil a national language in the northern and eastern provinces, where the Tamil were in the majority. But the language issue fanned an ethnic conflict that would continue for decades.

◉ The Modern Era

A Buddhist monk assassinated Prime Minister Bandaranaike in 1959. His widow, Sirimavo, won the 1960 elections and became the first woman in the world to serve as prime minister. She continued to pursue the ideas supported by her husband, but her government faced economic difficulties as well as ethnic clashes.

In 1965 Dudley Senanayake succeeded Sirimavo Bandaranaike, and his UNP administration imposed states of emergency, which increased ethnic tensions. Elections in 1970 returned Bandaranaike to office, but

Sirimavo Bandaranaike became the seventh prime minister of Ceylon in 1960. She was the first woman in the country to hold this position.

she faced a rebel youth movement, called the Janatha Vimukthi Peramuna (People's Liberation Front). The movement's leaders, who were Communists, sought to overthrow the SLFP government because they felt that Communism would solve Ceylon's economic and cultural problems. By the time the government suppressed the youth revolt in late 1971, thousands of Ceylonese had been killed. The prime minister declared a state of emergency. It remained in effect for six years.

In 1972 the Ceylonese legislature adopted a new constitution. It renamed Ceylon the Socialist Republic of Sri Lanka. Although it eliminated the British-held post of governor-general, the constitution left Sri Lanka within the British Commonwealth.

By mid-1973, the Tamil minority in the north had begun to demand a separate, independent state. No longer highly placed throughout Sri Lanka's civil service and educational system, the Tamil felt discriminated against in public employment, in university entrance, and in land grants. The two major Tamil political parties jointly formed the Tamil United Front (TUF). It aimed to protect and promote Tamil interests and to resolve Tamil grievances. The TUF eventually changed its name to the Tamil United Liberation Front (TULF) and actively supported the idea of Tamil Eelam—the name of the proposed independent nation.

The Liberation Tigers of Tamil Eelam (also known as the Tamil Tigers or the LTTE) is Sri Lanka's main group of separatists. This group is seeking self-rule for Sri Lanka's Tamil population.

In addition to creating the Sri Lankan republic, Sri Lanka's constitution introduced the office of executive president, although the prime minister still possessed great political power. In the election campaign of 1977, the UNP advocated a much stronger role for the president. Under the leadership of J. R. Jayewardene, the party won the elections

J. R. Jayewardene was Sri Lanka's first executive president.

In the 1980s, many **Tamil-owned buildings in Colombo burned down** during the civil war. Sinhalese members of Sri Lanka's army may have been responsible.

and passed another constitution that reorganized the executive branch. The document gave more political power to the president, who would be directly elected. The constitution also changed the name of the country to the Democratic Socialist Republic of Sri Lanka.

◉ Civil Strife

Throughout the 1980s, Sri Lanka was in a state of civil war. The Tamil rebellion, led by guerrillas and aimed at civilian as well as military targets, disrupted the northern third of the country. The disturbances caused conflicts even within the Sinhalese majority. Some Sinhalese wanted to negotiate an agreement, while others favored a military solution.

Despite the president's attempts in 1984 and 1985 to develop a dialogue with formal Tamil political parties, Tamil guerrilla groups continued to fight. In response, Sri Lanka's army began to take revenge on civilian Tamil populations.

In the late 1980s, the government of India stepped in to try to help solve the conflict by sending in a twenty-thousand-person peacekeeping force. The Indian troops sought to disarm the rebels and to quiet the violence, but their efforts met with little success. The Indians soon were fighting a war outside their borders.

In 1988 Sri Lankan national elections brought Ranasinghe Premadasa of the UNP to the presidency. After ordering the Indian forces to leave the island in early 1990, Premadasa tried to establish a cease-fire and to reopen negotiations for a compromise settlement with the Tamil guerrillas. The cease-fire quickly fell apart, and Premadasa was assassinated in 1993.

In the next year, the UNP began to lose popularity as more voters turned toward the People's Alliance. This new coalition, which included the SLFP, favored negotiations with the Tamil guerrillas. After the People's Alliance won a slight majority in legislative elections, Chandrika Bandaranaike Kumaratunga (the People's Alliance leader and the daughter of S. W. R. D. and Sirimavo Bandaranaike) became the new Sri Lankan prime minister. Shortly after that, Sri Lankans elected Kumaratunga as their president.

The People's Alliance said that it was committed to restoring peace in Sri Lanka. Peace talks got under way shortly after Kumaratunga took office, and in 1995 the government and the Tamil guerrillas agreed to a cease-fire. But peace talks broke down that April, and fighting soon resumed. Later that year, government troops overtook the Jaffna Peninsula, displacing the Tamil who lived there.

When **Chandrika Kumaratunga** became president of Sri Lanka in 1994, she became the first woman in the country to hold this political office. She appointed her mother—Sirimavo Bandaranaike—as prime minister.

In January 1998, Jaffna held its first local elections in fifteen years. In the spring, Jaffna's newly elected mayor was assassinated. Because the mayor was part of a pro-government group, many people suspected that the Tamil rebels were responsible for the assassination. Tensions continued in 1999, when a suicide bomber attempted to assassinate Kumaratunga in the days leading up to Sri Lanka's presidential elections. The attempt was unsuccessful, but the president did sustain injuries in the attack. Shortly after the assassination attempt, the people of Sri Lanka reelected Kumaratunga as their president.

In the spring of 2000, Tamil guerrillas overtook the Elephant Pass military complex on the Jaffna Peninsula—a significant victory that posed a grave threat to the Sri Lankan army. In response to the increasing tension and violence, a Norwegian peace envoy stepped in later that year to work for a compromise between the two sides. By December 2001, the government and the Tamil guerrillas agreed to a one-month cease-fire. The next year, they signed a permanent cease-fire agreement.

The cease-fire agreement led to positive results in Sri Lanka. Both sides released prisoners of war, and the road connecting the Jaffna Peninsula to the rest of Sri Lanka reopened. But the Tamil rebels still felt that they were being treated unfairly. In 2003 they withdrew from peace talks.

In late 2003, Kumaratunga and Ranil Wickremesinghe, Sri Lanka's prime minister, had a political disagreement. As a result, Kumaratunga dissolved Parliament in early 2004 and held elections in the spring of that year. A coalition called the United People's Freedom

WHY NORWAY? THE NORWEGIAN MODEL

Beginning in 1998, both the Tamil rebels and the Sri Lankan government sought Norway to mediate their dispute. Representatives of this small northern European nation of 4.5 million people have worked to resolve conflicts in the Middle East, Colombia, Guatemala, and Sudan. Norway's strategy of getting government and private groups or institutions to cooperate in seeking peaceful solutions has become known as the Norwegian Model.

Norwegians are united in their dedication to conflict resolution. The peace process for Sri Lanka has continued under three different Norwegian governments. As Kristin Halvorsen, leader of Norway's Socialist Left Party, puts it, "This is an issue above party politics . . . we want the efforts to succeed."

Alliance won control of Parliament, and Mahinda Rajapakse became prime minister. In July 2004, a suicide bombing in Colombo threatened to unravel Sri Lanka's peace process entirely.

Strife continued following the 2004 tsunami. The Sri Lankan government gave aid to help Sri Lankans recover from the disaster, but many Tamil separatists felt that the government did not evenly distribute the aid. They believed that the government neglected areas under separatist control. The government has denied these accusations. In June 2005, Tamil separatists and the Sri Lankan government took a step toward compromise—both sides signed an agreement to share international aid.

In August 2005, Sri Lanka's peace process suffered another apparent setback when the country's 73-year-old foreign minister, Lakshman Kadirgamar, was assassinated at his home in Colombo. Kadirgamar, an ethnic Tamil, was a senior official in President Kumaratunga's administration. While Kadirgamar's assassination spurred tensions in Sri Lanka, it did not lead to civil war as some had feared. Less than a week after the assassination, the Tamil separatists agreed to hold talks with the Sri Lankan government. The government, however, did not agree to meet with the separatists in Oslo, Norway, the separatists' favored location. Instead, the government insisted that the issues should be resolved in Sri Lanka.

The government and the Tamil nationalists continue to disagree on many issues. Kumaratunga remains president of the conflicted island, though her term is set to end in December 2005. While the cease-fire between the Tamil separatists still holds, the situation remains unstable.

Visit www.vgsbooks.com for links to websites publishing the most up-to-date news from Sri Lanka.

Government

Sri Lanka operates under an elected presidential system of government. The country adopted this system in 1978, after J. R. Jayewardene passed a new constitution. The executive president, who is also chief of state and commander of the armed forces, is elected directly by the people to a six-year term. The president is responsible to Parliament for the exercise of presidential duties and may be removed from office by a two-thirds majority vote of the legislature.

The president appoints the prime minister, who is the leader of the ruling party in the legislature and the head of the cabinet. The

Sri Lanka's Parliament building, located in Sri Jayawardenepura Kotte, is built on an island surrounded by an artifical lake created by draining a swamp. Top Sri Lankan architect Geoffrey Bawa accepted the commission to design it in 1979 and earned international praise. Bawa's work combines architectural elements of different places and time periods. He designed commercial buildings and religious and cultural structures as well.

president also appoints other cabinet ministers, deputy ministers, and noncabinet ministers. Parliament is a unicameral (one-house) body of 225 members who are elected to six-year terms by Sri Lankans eighteen years of age or older.

Sri Lanka's judiciary system consists of a supreme court, a court of appeals, a high court, and a number of lower courts. Parliament may create additional tribunals and may amend judiciary powers.

The legal system is a reflection of past colonial and cultural influences. For example, criminal laws follow the same framework as British laws, while civil law is of Roman-Dutch origin. Personal laws—relating to marriage, divorce, and inheritance—are unique to each ethnic group on the island. Kandyan law, for instance, applies to the Central Highlands, Thesavalamai law is for the northern Tamil community, and Muslims are governed by an Islamic code.

Sri Lanka is divided into twenty-five administrative districts. A government agent, who is a member of the Sri Lankan civil service, is responsible for all government activities in the district. Regional, city, and village councils are elected locally.

THE PEOPLE

More than 19 million people live in Sri Lanka. Approximately 79 percent of these people live in rural areas, with many residing in the Wet Zone where agricultural conditions are most favorable. The urban areas of Sri Lanka, where the most job opportunities exist, are home to roughly 21 percent of the population.

Although legally discouraged, some remnants of a caste system—which separates society into rigid social and professional classes—still exist in Sri Lanka, particularly in rural areas. Members of one family traditionally remain in the same caste, and marriages are often arranged within a caste. Although Buddhism rejects social barriers, Sinhalese Buddhists live by caste rules. In the Sinhalese caste system, farmers are of the highest standing, followed by craftspeople, fishers, clothes washers, and people of various other occupations. Hinduism includes a caste system, but the Sri Lankan Tamil follow an arrangement that is different from the one supported by the Tamil in India. With the spread of education,

caste differences are disappearing, especially in job selection and work opportunities.

Ethnic Groups

In Sri Lankan society, many languages, ethnic groups, and religions exist side by side. The Sinhalese are the major ethnic community, making up about 74 percent of the population. They are primarily Buddhists, but some are Christians. Two different Sinhalese groups—one in the highlands and the other in the low country—live in Sri Lanka.

Because of their relative isolation from European influences and developments, highland Sinhalese tend to be socially and politically conservative. The low-country Sinhalese—who have constantly been in contact with new cultures arriving on the coasts—tend to have a more liberal outlook. Many Sinhalese of both groups are farmers who raise rice and other crops in villages.

WANNIYALA-AETTO

Wanniyala-aetto means "Forest Dwellers." But most Sri Lankans don't use this word to describe their country's native people. Instead, they use the Sinhalese word *Vedda*, which implies "uncivilized." The Wanniyala-aetto have faced centuries of hardship. In 1983 the Sri Lankan government turned their hunting grounds into a national park. Because the grounds serve as a wildlife sanctuary, the Wanniyala-aetto were not permitted to hunt there. Furthermore, the grounds were home to several villages. Most of these villages were displaced when the park was created. Through the years, the Sri Lankan government has allowed the Wanniyala-aetto greater access to the park. But the Wanniyala-aetto still are not permitted to live freely on their native land.

The Tamil compose about 18 percent of the population and are mostly Hindus. The majority of these people are Sri Lankan Tamil, whose ancestors have lived on the island (especially in northern areas of the Jaffna Peninsula) for many centuries. They are involved in trade and other business activities in major cities, and some hold prominent government jobs throughout Sri Lanka. About 5 percent of the Tamil are Indian Tamil—the descendents of southern Indians who worked on the British-owned tea plantations in the nineteenth century. Many Indian Tamil still make their livelihoods in the central tea estates.

Other minority groups are the Malays (from present-day Malaysia), the Moors (people of Arab ancestry), and the Burghers (descendants of colonists from the Netherlands, Portugal, and the United Kingdom). A very small number of native Sri Lankans, called the Wanniyala-aetto, live in remote communities on the island. Some argue that the Wanniyala-aetto can no longer claim a distinct identity because they've become so integrated into village life. Together, these groups make up about 8 percent of the population.

◉ Language

In 1956 the government made Sinhala the official language of Sri Lanka. More than 70 percent of the population speaks Sinhala. After demonstrations by the Tamil minority, the government made Tamil a national language in 1978. Tamil is the language used in all administrative affairs of the northern and eastern provinces. Use of English—the official language under British rule—has been in decline since Sri Lanka achieved independence from Britain in 1948. In many upper-middle-class urban neighborhoods, however, English is still the primary language.

Sinhala uses written symbols derived from the Brahmi script of ancient Indian languages. One letter does not necessarily represent a single sound but instead may stand for a consonant and a vowel together. There are fifty-six letters in the language of Sinhala, and its spoken and written forms differ. Sinhala also has different dialects, or regional variations. The Sinhalese in the coastal areas of Sri Lanka may use different words and intonations (tones of voice) than the Sinhalese in the Central Highlands. Tamil, which is part of the South Indian Dravidian language group, has its own script. The Tamil script is also derived from Brahmi, but it is quite distinct from Sinhala. Tamil is spoken in many countries throughout Asia, including India, Malaysia, and Singapore.

Home and Family

Most of Sri Lanka's predominantly rural population lives in villages made up of small dwellings. Thousands of these villages are scattered throughout the country. The *cadjan* is a traditional rural housing style. These homes consist of wooden frames covered by mats made of woven coconut fronds, or leaves. Mud is a common building material in Sri Lanka. Mud homes keep their occupants cool, so they are well-suited to the island's warm climate. Mud homes also stand up to common pests, such as termites. People living in urban areas often reside in one-story houses that are crowded together. Many of these homes feature gardens in the backyard. Other urban residents live in apartment buildings constructed by the government in response to population growth in the cities.

Hedges partition this hillside into homes with gardens in Nuwara Eliya.

The 2004 tsunami created a large-scale housing crisis in Sri Lanka. The disaster left hundreds of thousands without homes. Rebuilding proved difficult in the months following the tsunami, as the Sri Lankan government passed laws banning the building of homes near the southern and eastern coasts. The government cited safety as its reason for passing laws regarding land use. However, some Sri Lankans claim that the government's goal was to eliminate shacks along the coasts in order to make these areas more appealing to hotel developers.

Village and family life are important in Sri Lanka. Families are typically close-knit, and large groups of relatives often live together. Sri Lankans have a great deal of respect for the elderly. Parents teach their children to look up to older family members, and children show special care and concern for their grandparents. When older family members need help with household tasks or personal care, their grown children usually provide it. Older people often live with their extended families instead of in retirement communities.

The birth of a baby is a particularly joyous occasion in a Sri Lankan family. Babies and young children typically receive a great deal of attention. Grandparents, aunts, uncles, and cousins shower new babies with gifts. Relatives join in throughout children's lives to help them celebrate important occasions and milestones.

In Sri Lanka, many people—especially villagers—continue to dress traditionally. Men wear **sarongs** (wraparound garments that form long skirts). Women dress in saris, large pieces of cloth that are wrapped around the waist to form long skirts and then draped over one shoulder. Women wear blouses underneath their saris.

Marriages also hold great importance for families. It is not uncommon for a Sri Lankan wedding celebration to go on throughout the night. Many marriage celebrations take place in the village. If the bride and groom are wealthy, they may throw their party in a lavish hotel. Tamil couples typically wed in temples, while Muslim ceremonies take place in the home of the bride. People of European descent usually wed in churches and follow the ceremony with a reception. Astrologers often have a hand in Sinhalese wedding plans. Astrologers choose the most favorable times for each step in the marriage process.

Arranged marriages are the tradition in Sri Lanka—although many men and women marry without extensive input from their families. Class and caste are important factors when it comes to choosing a spouse. Men and women may be matched according to their family's economic status and societal position.

Women traditionally take on the role of the caregiver in Sri Lankan families. While women in Sri Lanka have access to education and boast high levels of literacy, they often do not have the same level of independence as men. Customarily, Sri Lankan women perform housework and look after their children, while men serve as the protectors and breadwinners of their families. Increasingly, Sri Lankan women are taking jobs outside of the home. But when a woman has a baby, she often leaves her job to care for her child.

⊙ Health

Although health conditions in Sri Lanka are excellent compared to those in other southern Asian countries, differences exist between urban and rural areas. The higher

DOMESTIC WORKERS

While many Sri Lankan women work as homemakers, others must leave their families and work abroad in order to earn enough money to survive. Most of these workers take on menial jobs, putting in long hours as maids, cooks, or dishwashers. In addition, they often suffer abuse at the hands of their employers. Rape and other forms of assault are common. Although they perform hard labor and get very little time off, domestic workers do not earn much money. But the shortage of jobs and livable wages in Sri Lanka mean that many women are willing to serve as domestic workers.

standard of living in the cities, where the availability of good medical care is greater, is evident in low infant mortality rates and long life expectancy. Nationwide, life expectancy in Sri Lanka is 72 years, and the infant mortality rate is 10 deaths per 1,000 live births. Both figures compare favorably with other nations in the region.

Sri Lankans have good health care in part because the government pays for medical services. The government provides health care for all Sri Lankans through a large network of hospitals and other providers. In addition, the government has launched public health campaigns to educate citizens about family planning and other forms of preventive care. Widespread campaigns aimed at curing tuberculosis, malaria, and childhood diseases have also bettered health conditions throughout the nation. Sri Lanka was one of the first countries in the developing world to eradicate malaria. Nevertheless, ailments spread by impure food and water are common. Sri Lanka has a shortage of doctors, and rapid population growth has made it difficult for the nation's health department to keep pace with the need for new sewage and water systems. The 2004 tsunami increased the level of contamination in wells throughout Sri Lanka.

For those with the means to pay for their own health care, Sri Lanka has private clinics and hospitals. Some rural Sri Lankans add practitioners of Ayurveda to the medical personnel who take care of their health-care needs. Ayurvedic physicians use traditional herbal medicines to treat the sick, and registered Ayurvedics are recognized by the government's Ministry of Health.

For population statistics, health care updates, and other information about the people and social issues of Sri Lanka, visit www.vgsbooks.com for links.

This **United Nations tent colony,** about 56 miles (90 km) south of Colombo, was one of many erected to house the homeless after the 2004 tsunami. A thirteen-year-old resident of this tent colony washes her clothes at a water pump. She attends school in a tent too.

Education

Before the Europeans came, Buddhist monks were responsible for most educational training. Later, the Portuguese established Roman Catholic schools, and the Dutch organized Protestant institutions. Although the British founded many Protestant missions, the colonial government also provided financial support to schools of the Buddhist and Hindu faiths. The instructors taught in English, however, at the expense of the student's knowledge of local languages and cultures.

After independence, the government developed a system of free education from kindergarten through the university level, with Sinhala as the first language and English as a compulsory second language. Tamil children were educated in Tamil from primary through university classes.

School attendance is compulsory for children from the ages of five to fifteen, and a large number of children continue their studies until they are eighteen years old. As a result, Sri Lanka has a high literacy rate. About 90 percent of the population can read and write—a figure that compares extremely favorably with other developing nations.

Both private and state-run schools exist in Sri Lanka, although state-run schools are more numerous. Private schools, such as the Buddhist *pirivenas*, include their own subjects—Buddhist studies, for example—but must comply with national laws regarding educational content in order to receive state funds. The main institution of higher learning was the University of Ceylon until the 1970s, when its branch campuses became nine independent universities.

CULTURAL LIFE

Sri Lanka enjoys a rich and varied cultural life. From festivals and drama to sculpture and architecture, the island's people have embraced the arts for thousands of years. Cultural institutions such as museums, temples, and mosques line the streets in Colombo, and artisans in many parts of the country sell masks, baskets, and jewelry. The people of Sri Lanka have upheld their artistic heritage throughout their nation's history, and Sri Lanka's cultural traditions endure into the twenty-first century.

◉ Religion and Festivals

About 70 percent of Sri Lanka's population is Buddhist. The form of Buddhism practiced in Sri Lanka is known as Theravada Buddhism. (Theravada means teachings of the elders.) Buddhism is not a religion in the strict sense of the word. Instead of focusing on a deity (or god), Buddhism focuses on a way of life.

The underlying belief of Buddhism is that human suffering arises from the selfish desire for comfort and luxury. As laid down by Gautama

Buddha—who founded Buddhism in India in the sixth century B.C.—the way to put an end to desire is to follow eight rules of conduct. In Buddhist thought, *bhikkus*—monks who reject luxury and who follow this eightfold path—are the only people who will be able to achieve the highest state of understanding, called nirvana. A group of bhikkus forms a sangha, historically among the most important social and philosophical organizations in Sri Lanka. Bhikkus live according to the strictest interpretation of Theravada Buddhism, but ordinary people follow the Buddhist faith to a lesser degree and worship many regional gods, mainly of Hindu origin.

The strong sense of Buddhist family unity is clearly displayed during the festivals associated with New Year's Day in mid-April. Buddhists wear new clothes, beat traditional brass drums (rabanas), set off fireworks, and eat special delicacies. Believers look for good omens when they light the first hearth fire and when they eat the first meal of the new year.

In this **perahera in Kandy,** costumed domesticated elephants with tusks play important roles. Sri Lankans refer to this kind of elephant as a tusker.

In late July or in August, depending on when the full moon falls, several of the nation's many peraheras are held. The most important of these Buddhist processions takes place every year in Kandy. It is a formal parade for the sacred tooth relic of Gautama Buddha, which is housed in a temple in Kandy. According to legend, in the third century A.D., a princess hid the tooth in her hair to smuggle it out of India, which had become hostile to Buddhism. Faithful Buddhists carry the tooth through Kandy's streets, accompanied by brightly decorated elephants, flashy drums, traditional dancers, and colorful flowers.

About 15 percent of Sri Lanka's population is Hindu. Most Tamil practice Hinduism and worship several gods. The most important are Brahma, Shiva, and Vishnu. They also accept the four Vedas (collections of sacred hymns) as Hindu religious writings, worship cows as symbols of holiness and purity, and live under a caste system. Much of daily Hindu worship in Sri Lanka takes place within the home. But temples are the focus for the more important annual rituals, such as the New Year and Dewali. Dewali—also known as the Festival of Lights—is a highly significant holiday for Hindus. Dewali festivities

The colorful carvings on the **roof of a Hindu temple** in Maradankadawala, Sri Lanka, are about one or more of Hinduism's several gods.

usually occur in late October or early November. Hindus light thousands of oil lamps to celebrate the victory of good over evil and to welcome Lakshmi, the goddess of wealth.

About 8 percent of the population—both Sinhalese and Tamil—are Christians, mainly Roman Catholics. The Christian faith has existed in Sri Lanka since the arrival of the Portuguese, who converted many coastal peoples. Protestantism arrived with the Dutch and the British, but missionary efforts failed to develop a large Protestant community on the island. Christians in Sri Lanka celebrate their traditions much as they do in North America or Europe. They attend special church services around the Easter holiday, and they celebrate Christmas by singing festive carols and watching plays that tell the story of Jesus' birth. Many Christian families take their children to see Santa Claus in Sri Lanka's department stores.

The Islamic religion, founded in Arabia in the seventh century A.D., arrived in Sri Lanka with Arab traders. Sri Lanka's Muslims come from Malay and Moor populations. Approximately 7 percent of Sri Lanka's population, mostly in the coastal regions, follow Islam. Significant Islamic holidays include the Holy Prophet's Birthday, the month of Ramadan (in which Muslims fast from sunrise to sunset), and a large feast at the end of Ramadan.

Architecture and the Arts

Ancient Sinhalese sculpture and architecture stretch over a 1,500-year period. The cities of Anuradhapura and Polonnaruwa are home to some of the world's greatest architectural treasures. Highly skilled artisans carved gigantic statues, stupas, and the entrances to palaces and temples. Massive shrines contrast with delicate art forms, like those used to make the pillars of Nissanka Latha Mandapaya pavillion. These are carved in the shape of lotus blossoms.

The oldest remaining examples of early painting—and the only ones that do not deal with religious subjects—are at Sigiriya, west of Polonnaruwa. The frescoes (painting on plaster) portray large-eyed women with faint smiles in subtle shades of red, yellow, and green.

Modern schools of painting and sculpture have experimented with impressionist and abstract styles that use both European and local themes. Artists, such as Senaka Senanayake and Tissa Ranasinghe, have exhibited internationally. Some have received commissions (money paid to them for their work) from Sri Lankan businesses, from Buddhist temples, and occasionally from the government.

Cottage industries, in which artists make craft products in their homes or in village workshops, are an important aspect of Sri Lankan life. Most Sinhalese craftspeople live in small villages, and their output is of considerable value to the economy of the country.

Masks are a common craft item throughout Sri Lanka. They serve several important cultural functions. Performers wear masks in a

Not all masks crafted in Sri Lanka are sold to tourists. This **traditional devil dancer** wears a mask and costume for a live demonstration of the use of masks in Sri Lankan culture.

A **man selling straw hats in Hikkaduwa, Sri Lanka,** sits patiently with his merchandise.

special type of drama in which all the players dress in costume. Celebrants wear masks at Sri Lanka's numerous religious processions and festivals. And devil dancers wear masks to impersonate—and thereby drive out—demons.

Artists sell carefully crafted masks in various shops, many of which the government runs. Toys, walking sticks, and ashtrays covered with a shiny varnish, called lacquer, are famous throughout Sri Lanka too. Artisans produce delicate handmade lace in Galle. Kalutara, south of Colombo, is renowned for its baskets, sandals, sun hats, table mats, and other woven objects.

As arts and crafts sales are an important source of revenue for the country, the Sri Lankan government encourages such enterprises. It supports training schools, and it assists artists in finding raw materials to make their crafts and markets in which to sell them.

◑ Literature

The literature of Sri Lanka goes back to the third century B.C., when Mahendra, an Indian prince, introduced Buddhism to the island. The written tradition includes ancient chronicles—such as the *Mahavamsa*—which preserve religious and historical events.

Pali—the northern Indian language used to record Buddhist teachings and traditions—continues to be the classical language of Theravada Buddhism in Sri Lanka. Most early Sinhalese literature is based on translations of works originally composed in Pali.

In time, the Sinhalese developed their own literature. Among the best-known literary classics are the thirteenth-century *Kavsilumina,* a long romantic poem, and collections of writings, called *Jatakas,* concerning the life of Buddha.

The modern era produced many Sinhalese novelists, such as Piyadasa Sirisena, who brought nationalist themes to their work. Others, such as W. A. Silva, were famous for their ability to tell a good story, often based on historical events. In the late twentieth century, some novelists began to write about current issues, such as modernization versus tradition in Sri Lankan society. Novelist Michael Ondaatje, who is of Dutch descent, addresses postcolonial issues in his writing. Ondaatje was born in Sri Lanka but immigrated to Great Britain as a child and eventually relocated to Canada. He is the author of many books and is best known for his 1992 novel *The English Patient*, which was made into an Academy award-winning film. Other works by Ondaatje include *Running in the Family* (a memoir he penned after returning to his native Sri Lanka) and *Anil's Ghost* (a novel set in Sri Lanka during the civil war).

Food

Rice is the basis of the daily Sri Lankan diet. A heaping dish of rice and curry (a food that is seasoned with a blend of strong spices of the same name) is the customary main meal of the day for rural residents. Sri Lankans often serve curry and rice with fruit as a second course. Roti is another common dish. Roti is a flat bread served with curry.

In Sri Lanka's urban areas, many professionals don't have time to sit down for a large meal. Instead, they often purchase lunch packets, sold by street vendors throughout the nation. Lunch packets are bundles of rice and curry. They usually include curried vegetables, a spicy side dish called a *sambol*, and either an egg or a helping of fish, beef, or chicken.

Treats called hoppers make delicious breakfasts in Sri Lanka. Hoppers are a hot, pancakelike food that is cooked over a flame and often served with curries, yogurt, or honey. Although hoppers are typically a breakfast food, they also make hearty and delicious snacks.

Tea is served with most Sri Lankan meals as a refreshment. Other drinks include fruit juice, *kurumba* (water from a green coconut), and *tambili* (water from the golden-colored king coconut). Most Buddhists obey the religious ban against eating meat, but they often consume fish with rice and curry. A great variety of seasonings add diversity to the curries, and a wide range of fruits—such as bananas, coconuts, mangoes, papayas, oranges, pineapples, and pomegranates—supplements plain rice.

A Sri Lankan vendor cuts open a golden-colored king coconut for a customer in Unawatuna. The king coconut's juice, called tambili, makes an appealing drink in regions where drinking water may be polluted. Until the coconut is opened, tambili is pure as well as sweet. Only a clean knife is needed to keep it pure.

KIRI BATH

Kiri bath, or rice cooked in coconut milk, is a favorite Sri Lankan dish. Sri Lankans traditionally serve this treat at weddings and on other festive occasions. It is also often the first solid food fed to infants.

3 cups water

2 cups short-grain white rice

2 cups coconut milk

2 teaspoons salt

2 teaspoons ground cinnamon (optional)

1. Bring water to a boil. Add rice and cook on low heat for about 15 minutes.
2. Add coconut milk, salt, and cinnamon (if desired), and stir until well blended.
3. Cover pan and cook on low heat until milk is absorbed (about 10 to 15 minutes).
4. Spread the rice onto a flat dish. Cut the rice into squares and serve.

Serves 4

Sri Lankan cuisine has absorbed elements from its many influential cultures. As a result, Dutch foods such as *broeder* (a Christmas cake) and *lamprai* (a rice dish) have found their way into Sri Lanka's cooking, as have Portuguese cookies, known as *boroa*. Tamil traditions include *thosai* (pancakes) and *vade* (spicy doughnuts), and many Malay Muslims make *wattalapam*—coconut milk pudding.

Sports and Recreation

In Sri Lanka, people young and old follow the game of cricket. This British game is similar to baseball. British colonizers imported the sport to the island nation. When Sri Lanka's national cricket team plays, fans from all over the country show up to cheer on their team, while others stop what they are doing to tune in to radio broadcasts of the game. Cricket players are celebrities in Sri Lanka. Their names are well known in most Sri Lankan households, and many fans can recite statistics and other trivia about their favorite players.

In 1996 Sri Lankan cricket fans celebrated an historic victory. That year their national team won the World Cup in Lahore, Pakistan. After the win, cricket players gained even greater status in their home country. Advertisers hired them to endorse various products, and the Sri Lankan government showered them with gifts of land and money.

While cricket is a popular spectator sport, many Sri Lankans prefer to play the game themselves rather than tune in to broadcasts on radio or television. Amateur teams gather on Sundays to challenge other teams to matches. In many towns, children play impromptu games with makeshift bats and balls.

In addition to cricket, many Sri Lankans watch and play volley-ball, tennis, and soccer (known as football in Sri Lanka). They also enjoy track-and-field events. In the 1948 Olympic Games, Duncan White became one of Sri Lanka's top track-and-field stars when he earned a silver medal for his country in the men's 400-meter hurdle event. Traditional games are popular during holidays and national fes-tivals. In one traditional game, Sri Lankans try to climb poles slathered with grease in order to capture flags placed at the top. Many Sri Lankans play *panche*, in which players use shells as dice. British horse racing is another favorite pastime. Some Sri Lankans closely follow the horses and even place bets on them.

In large cities, many people visit movie theaters to see films from Sri Lanka, India, and Hollywood. They also attend puppet theater and plays. Almost everyone in Sri Lanka enjoys leisure reading. Novels, newspapers, and comic books are all popular among Sri Lankans, who place a high value on the written word. Sri Lankans tend to stay informed about current events. They pride themselves on knowing a great deal about their communities and the larger world.

Go to www.vgsbooks.com for links to websites about sports, art, literature, and cuisine in Sri Lanka.

THE ECONOMY

From colonial times to the twenty-first century, Sri Lanka has exported plantation crops, such as tea, coconut, and rubber, to countries around the world. These crops are an important part of Sri Lanka's economy, and many countries benefit from Sri Lanka's ability to export these items. Throughout the years, however, tumultuous political conditions have hurt the nation's financial outlook. Factors such as unemployment and ethnic strife have prevented Sri Lanka from realizing its full economic potential.

In spite of the civil unrest, Sri Lanka's economy appeared to be improving in the late 1990s. By 2000, however, ethnic struggles once again cast a shadow over the country's financial picture. The economy recovered briefly around 2001. But by the middle of that year, an attack at the Colombo airport led to increasing instability in Sri Lanka and discouraged foreign investors from doing business with the nation. In September 2001, terrorist attacks against the United States caused an economic slowdown around the world. Tourism decreased due to

fears of terrorism, and demand for textiles and apparel (another main-stay of Sri Lanka's economy) dropped substantially. For the first time, Sri Lanka's economy shrank.

In 2002 a formal cease-fire was declared between the Sri Lankan government and Tamil separatists. As a result of the cease-fire, tourism increased, as did exports of crops and textiles. For the next few years, Sri Lanka saw an increase in its gross domestic product (GDP, the value of goods and services produced in Sri Lanka each year). But uncertainty over the peace process detered foreign investors, and the 2004 tsunami further threatened Sri Lanka's economy. The crucial tourism industry was hurt, as were agriculture and the fishing industry. The long-term economic effects of the tsunami have yet to be seen.

◉ Tourism

Sri Lanka's services sector—of which tourism is a crucial part—accounts for about 54 percent of the nation's GDP and employs

TOURISM ZONES

As part of its campaign to increase tourism to Sri Lanka, the Sri Lankan government has worked to establish several tourism zones throughout the country. Tourism zones are areas set aside for the development of upscale resorts and hotels. The government's plans call for the development of fifteen such zones.

While upscale accommodations are likely to increase Sri Lanka's tourism revenues, the government's rebuilding plan is controversial. Many small-business proprietors who lost their hotels or guesthouses in the tsunami may not be able to rebuild within the tourism zones. As a result, some local hotel owners may lose their businesses.

approximately 42 percent of the workforce. Tourism is an important industry in Sri Lanka, and the island's leaders have spent many years developing the tourist trade. The government created the Ceylon Tourist Board in 1966 to expand and improve the nation's facilities for visitors. In the decades that followed, the board oversaw the construction of guesthouses and hotels in all the major cities and in most towns.

Sri Lanka offers the visitor good communications and transport, a variety of natural scenery, a magnificent array of architectural treasures from the past, and the pageantry of an ancient culture. In addition, Sri Lanka has well-developed recreational facilities for golfing, spearfishing, skin diving, surfing, sunbathing, and mountain climbing. Visitors to Sri Lanka's national parks can see many animals in their native habitats.

Despite these attractions, the civil war between government troops and the Tamil separatists has limited the nation's appeal as a tourist spot. In addition, the tsunami has adversely affected tourism, as many tourists were reluctant to travel to Sri Lanka immediately following the disaster. In an effort to bolster the tourism industry, the Sri Lankan government has undertaken a campaign to encourage people to vacation in Sri Lanka. The government's Task Force for Rebuilding the Nation joined with the Ministry of Tourism and the Ceylon Tourist Board in order to promote Sri Lanka as an ideal vacation destination.

Industry

Industry—which includes mining, quarrying, manufacturing, and construction—accounts for much of the economic growth in Sri Lanka. Statistics show that industry accounts for roughly 26 percent of the GDP and employs approximately 24 percent of the workforce. Apparel is a major part of manufacturing in Sri Lanka, and the

This **garment factory in Sri Lanka** employs 1,200 people.

clothing industry generates a great deal of revenue. A recent study showed that apparel and textile sales contribute more than 50 percent of Sri Lanka's export earnings (money earned from goods sent overseas). In addition to apparel and textiles, Sri Lankan factories produce food and beverages, petroleum products, and coal products.

Sri Lanka has limited mineral resources, except for large deposits of high-grade graphite. According to recent statistics, mining contributes just 1.8 percent of Sri Lanka's GDP. Other minerals in Sri Lanka include iron ore, monazite, uranium, clay, and ilmenite (a black ore). Limestone is extracted for a government-owned cement corporation at Kankesanturai on the Jaffna Peninsula. Gemstones are Sri Lanka's most important mineral export. The valleys around Ratnapura contain a wide variety of precious and semiprecious stones, including sapphires, rubies, garnets, aquamarines, moonstones, and topazes.

Agriculture

Agriculture (of which forestry and fishing are a part) accounts for about 20 percent of Sri Lanka's GDP and employs about 34 percent of the workforce. In volume, rice is the largest single domestic crop grown in Sri Lanka. Secondary crops include coconuts, sugarcane, and cassava, as well as spices such as cinnamon and pepper.

The 2004 tsunami drastically impacted Sri Lanka's rice crop. About 5,374 acres (2,175 hectares) of rice paddies were laid waste, and the ocean waters that washed up on the land left much of Sri Lanka's soil contaminated with salt. Crops cannot grow on land in which salt

Small family gardens are important sources of food crops and medicinal herbs. This garden far inland near Kandy escaped damage from the 2004 tsunami, but many of these precious gardens, as well as large agricultural plots, were lost.

levels are too high. Farm equipment also sustained damage in the disaster. Many tools used to cultivate rice and other crops were destroyed.

Animals are an important part of agriculture in Sri Lanka. Recent estimates show that Sri Lankan farmers raise more than 1 million cattle, 643,000 buffalo, 452,000 goats, and 73,000 pigs. Herders raise cattle for their milk, and they also use them as work animals.

Tea is a key crop, and Sri Lanka exports more tea than any other country in the world. Tea grows at many elevations. Plants at the highest altitudes are the choicest and bear the classification high grown if they come from slopes more than 4,000 feet (1,200 m) above sea level. Medium-grown tea is from bushes planted between 2,000 and 4,000 feet (600 to 1,200 m) high, and any tea from lower altitudes is called low grown. The government has transferred most of the state-owned tea estates to private owners.

Other primary exports include rubber and coconut. Rubber plantations lie in low, hot areas of the southwest, where the amount of rainfall is more than 80 inches (203 cm) annually. Like tea estates, most of the large rubber plantations have been privatized by the government.

Unlike tea and rubber, coconuts have a large market within Sri Lanka as well as abroad. Coconuts come from trees on small holdings primarily along the southwestern coast. The fruit contains a refreshing drink, and the coarse fibers (called coir) of the husk can be woven into bags or mats. The coconut's meat, called copra, may be shredded as a food. The meat can also be dried and processed into a useful oil.

The forests of Sri Lanka were once much larger than they are in the twenty-first century. Many acres of valuable native trees, such as the calamander, have been cleared to expand farming plots and pastureland. To offset the destruction of this natural resource, the government has sponsored reforestation schemes and has planted teak, eucalyptus, mahogany, and other commercially profitable trees.

Two kinds of fishing industries exist in Sri Lanka. A small inland industry based on reservoirs contributes to the daily diet of rural people. Ocean fishing in coastal areas that are not part of the nation's network of wildlife preserves is done on a larger scale. The fishing industry was significantly damaged by the tsunami. More than 100,000 fishers lost their jobs, and about 50 percent of the fishing vessels in 80 percent of the fishing areas were harmed. Foreign aid has helped some of the fishers restore their livelihoods.

In Weligama, Sri Lanka, locals have a unique technique for fishing. They wade out to **fish from stilts** embedded in the ocean floor. Many of these poles, handed down from father to son, were lost in the 2004 tsunami.

Trains on the Colombo-Kandy-Badulla route stop at Haputale. It is a small market town set among tea plantations.

Infrastructure

Roads and railways connect most regions in Sri Lanka. According to recent statistics, Sri Lanka has approximately 60,083 miles (96,694 km) of roads. Most of the roads are paved, but some are still narrow dirt tracks. More than 900 miles (1,449 km) of railways haul goods and transport people, while ferry services connect Sri Lanka with nearby India. The best roads and railways link the plantation areas to Colombo—the nation's main port.

On the local level, state-owned buses and private minibus services offer transport to local communities. In rural areas, animals pull carts, and people often travel on foot. Sri Lanka operates an international airport at Katunayake, near Colombo, and has several other major airports in the country. The major air carrier, SriLankan Airlines, provides domestic and international services on scheduled flights throughout the world.

Sri Lankans have more cellular telephones than main line telephones. There are about 931,600 cellular phones and 881,400 main

Check up on Sri Lanka's economic recovery from its civil war and from the tsunami of 2004. Go to www.vgsbooks.com for links.

line phones in use. About 200,000 Sri Lankans use the Internet, and 1,882 Internet hosts operate in the country.

Hydroelectricity provides nearly half of Sri Lanka's total energy. Imported oil and natural gas provide the balance of the country's energy needs.

◉ The Future

After more than four hundred years of colonial rule, Sri Lanka achieved independence without bloodshed. With fertile soil and a favorable agricultural climate, Sri Lanka nationalized many of its income-producing farms after independence, while attempting to develop and broaden its range of products for both domestic and foreign markets. Its system of rural and urban medical care has produced a high life expectancy and a low rate of infant morality. Yet, despite these beneficial changes, Sri Lanka continues to experience civil unrest.

Following the 2004 tsunami, Sri Lanka has been working to rebuild. Meanwhile, the internal conflict between government troops and the Tamil guerrillas has officially ended, but tensions still exist in the nation. Many Sri Lankans on both sides of the conflict have been displaced, and the fighting has claimed many lives. Sri Lanka's potential for future growth, stability, and prosperity depends on its ability to maintain peace.

CA. 500 B.C.	The Sinhalese arrive in Sri Lanka from mainland India. Vijaya, an exiled Indian prince, conquers the island's inhabitants and establishes the Sinhala kingdom.
200S B.C.	The son of the Indian emperor Asoka introduces Buddhism to Sri Lanka. The Tamil arrive in Sri Lanka from mainland India. Anuradhapura becomes a capital city.
A.D. 500S	Buddhist monks write the *Mahavamsa,* a chronicle of Sri Lanka.
1017	The Cholas capture the Sinhalese king Mahinda V and take him to India. They establish Polonnaruwa as their capital.
1070	Vijayabahu I, a Sinhalese prince, overthrows the Cholas and regains control of Anuradhapura. He retains Polonnaruwa as the kingdom's capital, thereby securing Sinhalese predominance in the southern and central regions.
CA. 1165	Sinhalese troops invade Myanmar.
1505	Portuguese navigators visit Sri Lanka in search of spices.
1597	The Portuguese assume formal rule of Sri Lanka.
1638	The Dutch drive the Portuguese out of Sri Lanka.
1796	The British capture the port of Trincomalee.
1802	The British declare their lands in Sri Lanka to be a colony.
1815	The British take control of Sri Lanka and begin developing large-scale agriculture.
1912	Nationalists organize a railway strike.
1915	The British declare martial law in Sri Lanka.
1919	The Ceylon National Congress is established.
1942	The British lose their port at Singapore, and Trincomalee regains its position as a strategic outpost.
1946	The postwar British government approves the first constitution in Sri Lanka.
1947	The British grant Sri Lanka commonwealth status.
1948	Sri Lanka achieves independence from Britain. D. S. Senanayake becomes the country's first prime minister.
1952	Senanayake dies in a horse-riding accident. Senanayake's son Dudley succeeds him as prime minister.
1953	Dudley Senanayake is forced to resign after riots break out.
1956	S. W. R. D. Bandaranaike is elected prime minister of Sri Lanka. Sinhala becomes Sri Lanka's official language.

1959   Bandaranaike is assassinated by a Buddhist monk.

1960   Bandaranaike's widow, Sirimavo, is elected prime minister.

1971   The Janatha Vimukthi Peramuna (People's Liberation Front) engages in riots in an attempt to overthrow the government.

1972   Sri Lanka's name changes from Ceylon to the Socialist Republic of Sri Lanka. Tamil separatists found the LTTE.

1973   The Tamil minority in northern Sri Lanka begin to demand a separate state.

1978   Sri Lanka adopts an elected presidential system of government. Tamil becomes a national language.

1983   Civil war begins between the Sri Lankan government and the Tamil separatists.

1987   India sends peacekeeping troops to Sri Lanka.

1988   Ranasinghe Premadasa is elected president of Sri Lanka.

1993   Premadasa is assassinated.

1994   Chandrika Kumaratunga is elected president of Sri Lanka.

1995   Peace talks between the Sri Lankan government and the Tamil separatists break down. Government troops force Tamil separatists out of the Jaffna Peninsula.

1996   The Sri Lankan cricket team wins the World Cup in Lahore, Pakistan.

1998   Jaffna's mayor is assassinated.

1999   A suicide bomber attempts to assassinate President Kumaratunga. Kumaratunga is reelected president.

2000   Tamil separatists capture the Elephant Pass. A Norwegian envoy works to establish peace between the Sri Lankan government and Tamil separatists.

2001   The government and Tamil separatists agree to a one-month cease-fire.

2002   The government and the Tamil separatists formally agree to a cease-fire.

2003   The Tamil separatists withdraw from peace talks.

2004   A suicide bombing in Colombo threatens the peace process. An Indian Ocean tsunami takes the lives of more than 30,000 Sri Lankans and leaves about 900,000 others without homes.

2005   Sri Lanka's foreign minister, Lakshman Kadirgamar, is assassinated. The Tamil separatists agree to hold talks with the Sri Lankan government in Oslo, Norway. The government, however, insists that issues be resolved in Sri Lanka, delaying the talks.

COUNTRY NAME Democratic Socialist Republic of Sri Lanka

AREA 25,332 square miles (65,610 sq. km)

MAIN LANDFORMS Coastal Lowlands, Central Highlands, Nuwara Eliya, Horton Plains, Hatton Plateau, Uva Basin, Adam's Peak, Rakwana Hills, Dolosbage Mountains

HIGHEST POINT Pidurutalagala (8,281 ft. or 2,524 m above sea level)

MAJOR RIVERS Mahaweli River, Kelani River, Kalu Oya, Aruvi Aru

ANIMALS elephants, bears, wild boars, leopards, cheetahs, deer, and buffalo

CAPITAL CITY Colombo

OTHER MAJOR CITIES Sri Jayawardenepura Kotte, Jaffna, Galle, Kandy, Trincomalee

OFFICIAL LANGUAGES Sinhala and Tamil

MONETARY UNIT Sri Lanka rupee, 100 cents=1 rupee.

Currency Fast Facts

SRI LANKA'S CURRENCY

Sri Lanka's standard unit of currency is the Sri Lanka rupee, with 100 cents in a rupee. Rupee notes come in denominations of 10, 20, 50, 100, 200, 500, and 1,000. The Central Bank of Sri Lanka issues all of Sri Lanka's currency.

Throughout the years, the Central Bank of Sri Lanka has minted many special coins to commemorate national events. In 1998, for example, the bank minted a coin marking the fiftieth anniversary of Sri Lanka's independence from Britain. In 1999 it issued a coin celebrating the Sri Lankan cricket team's 1996 World Cup victory. Other coins have honored various anniversaries and leaders in Sri Lanka.

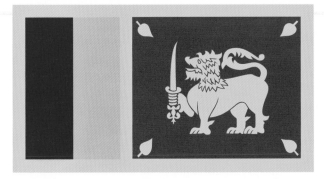

The design of the Sri Lankan flag became official in 1978, after the country changed its name from Ceylon to Sri Lanka. The flag features two panels outlined in yellow, one with vertical bands of green and orange and the other with a red rectangle and a sword-carrying lion. Each corner of the red rectangle features a yellow bo leaf.

The green and orange bands represent the island's Muslim and Hindu minorities, respectively. The lion carrying a sword is an ancient Kandyan image. The four leaves symbolize the sacred bo tree, under which the philosopher Gautama Buddha sat while gaining enlightenment.

The Sri Lankan national anthem was chosen on November 22, 1951. It was first played in 1952 on February 4, the fourth anniversary of Sri Lanka's independence. Following are the lyrics to the first stanza of the anthem.

Mother Lanka, we worship Thee!
Plenteous in prosperity, Thou,
Beauteous in grace and love,
Laden with corn and luscious fruit
And fragrant flowers of radiant hue,
Giver of life and all good things
Our land of joy and victory,
Receive our grateful praise sublime,
Lanka! We worship Thee!

 To listen to Sri Lanka's national anthem, go to www.vgsbooks.com for a link.

GUNADASA AMARASEKARA (b. 1929) This novelist, essayist, and poet was born in a village near Galle. A renowned literary figure, he created a new poetic form derived from the folk poems of Sri Lanka. His career began in the early 1950s, when he won an international short story contest sponsored by the *New York Herald Tribune*. He went on to revolutionize Sinhalese writing, penning stories and critiques on politicians, intellectuals, and the middle class. Amarasekara is a dentist by trade. He started writing while studying dentistry at the University of Peradeniya.

ARTHUR C. CLARKE (b. 1917) This well-known science fiction author and inventor was born in Minehead, Somerset, Great Britain. He has been a resident of Colombo since 1956. In 1964 he collaborated with film producer Stanley Kubrick to write the screenplay *2001: A Space Odyssey*. In addition to this work, he authored *Profiles of the Future, 2010: Odyssey Two*, and many other nonfiction and science fiction titles. He also has an interest in underwater diving. He owned a diving school along Sri Lanka's southern coast, but the school was destroyed in the 2004 tsunami.

VERNON COREA (1927–2002) Born in the town of Kurana, Corea gained fame as a radio broadcaster in Sri Lanka and Great Britain. Corea began working as a relief announcer for Radio Ceylon in 1957. In 1974 he became the director of news at the Sri Lanka Broadcasting Corporation. After moving to Great Britain in the mid-1970s, Corea worked for the BBC as an ethnic minorities adviser. In this position, Corea expanded multicultural radio programming and trained broadcasters from many ethnic backgrounds.

GAMINI FONSEKA (1936–2004) Fonseka was born in Dehiwala, Sri Lanka, and gained fame as an actor and film producer. Equally comfortable with artistic and popular movies, he had a large following in his home country and abroad. Fonseka started out as a film technician and went on to act in numerous pictures. He had a great deal of influence in the development of Sinhalese cinema. In addition to his film career, Fonseka was active in politics. He was a regional governor as well as a deputy speaker in Parliament.

SUSANTHIKA JAYASINGHE (b. 1975) This Olympic sprinter grew up in the impoverished village of Atnawala. As a young girl, she loved to race but couldn't afford spikes or running shoes. In 2000 she represented Sri Lanka at the Summer Olympics in Sydney, Australia. She won a bronze medal in the women's 200-meter final, becoming the first Sri Lankan in 52 years to medal at the Olympic Games. After her remarkable Olympic performance, she went on to earn a gold medal at the 2002 Asian Games in Pusan, South Korea.

SANATH JAYASURIYA (b. 1969) Jayasuriya was born in the city of Matara. He made a name for himself as a batsman on the Sri Lankan cricket team.

Known as the master blaster, Jayasuriya helped his team win the World Cup in 1996. After the win, Jayasuriya was named the tournament's Most Valuable Player. In 2001 Jayasuriya's hometown named a stadium after him. Jayasuriya presided over the stadium's grand opening.

CHANDRIKA BANDARANAIKE KUMARATUNGA (b. 1945) Born in Colombo, Kumaratunga is the daughter of prime ministers S. W. R. D. Bandaranaike and Sirimavo Bandaranaike. After earning a degree in political science from the University of Paris, Kumaratunga followed in her parents' footsteps and pursued a career in politics. Kumaratunga experienced many personal tragedies. Her father was assassinated when she was a child, and her husband, Wijaya Kumaratunga, was killed by political adversaries in 1988. Kumaratunga pursued her goals in spite of the hardships. In 1994 she rose to Sri Lanka's highest political office when she was elected president.

SWARNA MALLAWARACHCHI (b. ca. 1950) Born into poverty and sold as an orphan while still an infant, Mallawarachchi became one of Sri Lanka's leading film stars. She has acted in many pictures and won the country's best actress award nineteen times. Mallawarachchi also works as an activist. After the 2004 Indian Ocean tsunami, she toured Sri Lanka's refugee camps, encouraging women and girls to protect themselves from sexual violence in the shelters.

INDRANI PERERA (b. 1950) This popular singer lives in Rajagiriya, Sri Lanka. She joined a rock band called the Moonstones and went on to form a singing group with her sisters in 1969. She quickly rose to fame and decided to launch a solo career. She has recorded numerous albums and performed in cities throughout the world.

PRASANNA VITHANAGE (b. 1962) This acclaimed film director got his start in theater as a young man. In 1986 he translated and directed George Bernard Shaw's play *Arms and the Man*. He directed his first movie, *Sisila Gini Gani (Ice on Fire)*, in 1992. The picture won nine Sri Lankan film awards. Vithanage's most recent film, *Ira Madiyama (August Sun)*, deals with the war between the Tamil separatists and the Sri Lankan government. On May 19, 2005, the Cannes Film Festival screened the picture on a special day dedicated to Sri Lankan cinema.

CLARENCE WIJEWARDENE (1943–1996) Born in Haputale, Wijewardene was a well-known Sri Lankan musician. As a young man, Wijewardene formed a rock band. The band—eventually known as the Moonstones—was immensely popular in Sri Lanka. Wijewardene was a member of several bands throughout his life. He also performed as a solo artist and composed songs for film and television.

ADAM'S PEAK Located in Sri Lanka's hill country, this 7,360-foot (2,243 m) peak has been a place of religious pilgrimage for more than one thousand years. From the top of the mountain, the view of the hill country is remarkable. Many pilgrims climb Adam's Peak in the early hours of the morning to watch the sun rise from its summit.

ANURADHAPURA This city became Sri Lanka's capital in 380 B.C. It remained so until the tenth century A.D., when it was overthrown by the Cholas. Visitors to Anuradhapura can see stupas and museums, as well as the sacred bo tree—the oldest living tree in the world.

HORTON PLAINS The grasslands of the Horton Plains serve as a serene spot for hikers in Sri Lanka. Along with scattered evergreen forests, this destination features two scenic mountain peaks—Kirigalpotta and Totapola. Horton Plains also features a natural wonder known as World's End, where the plains plummet downward for 2,297 feet (700 meters).

KELANIYA RAJA MAHA VIHARA Located in Colombo, this temple is an important place of worship for people of the Buddhist faith. Buddhists believe that Gautama Buddha once preached at the site. The temple is also notable for its image of a reclining Buddha.

NATIONAL MUSEUM This museum in Colombo has been open to the public since 1877. It is home to collections of Sinhalese artwork, historic paintings, and valuable antiques. In addition to traditional exhibits, the building features a children's museum and a floor dedicated to the art of puppetry.

POLONNARUWA The Cholas adopted Polonnaruwa as their capital city in the eleventh century A.D. It was Sri Lanka's capital for more than two hundred years. Polonnaruwa features monuments constructed by the Cholas. The greatness of the monuments testifies to the ingenuity of their creators.

SRI KAILAWASANATHAR SWAMI DEVASTHANAM Located at Captain's Gardens in Colombo, this Hindu temple is the oldest—as well as one of the largest—in Sri Lanka. Visitors to this sacred place of Hindu worship can see shrines dedicated to the gods Shiva and Ganesh.

YALA NATIONAL PARK This nature reserve suffered some damage in the 2004 tsunami, but it remains one of the best places in Sri Lanka to see animals such as elephants, monkeys, buffalo, and boars. Yala also boasts a large population of birds, as well as a wide variety of natural features such as plains, lagoons, and scrubs.

Ayurveda: a traditional type of medicine in which physicians use herbs to treat the sick. In Sri Lanka, registered practitioners of Ayurveda are recognized by the government's Ministry of Health.

Buddhism: a religion founded in India by the philosopher Gautama Buddha. The ideals of Buddhism include the search for enlightenment, the rejection of worldly possessions, and a life of wisdom and virtue.

caste: a system of class that determines a person's social and professional standing. The caste system is legally discouraged in Sri Lanka, but it still wields influence in the country.

dynasty: a powerful family or group that rules over an area for an extended period of time

guerrilla: a person who employs irregular warfare or a movement made up of such people

Hinduism: a religion whose followers worship several gods, the most important of which are Brahma, Shiva, and Vishnu. Hindus also accept the four Vedas (collections of sacred hymns) as Hindu religious writings, worship cows as holy symbols, and live under a caste system.

Mahavamsa: a chronicle from the sixth century A.D. in which Buddhist monks wrote down what they knew about Sri Lanka. The *Mahavamsa* was written in Pali (a language that has its roots in the ancient Indian language of Sanskrit). The chronicle includes information about religious and ancient historical events.

missionary: a person on a religious mission, generally to promote a particular type of religion

monastery: a dwelling place for a person who has taken religious vows

monsoon: seasonal winds that bring heavy rainfall. Sri Lanka has two monsoon seasons, the southwest monsoon, between May and November, and the northeast monsoon, between December and February.

mosque: an Islamic place of worship

Sinhalese: the largest ethnic group in Sri Lanka. The Sinhalese are descendants of northern Indians.

Tamil: the second-largest ethnic group in Sri Lanka and the language spoken by this group. The Tamil trace their roots to southern India.

tsunami: an ocean wave produced by earth movement, such as an earthquake

Selected Bibliography

Arnold, Elizabeth. "Nature Bounces Back on Sri Lanka's Coast." *National Public Radio.* February 25, 2005.
http://www.npr.org/templates.story/story.php?storyId=4511322 (May 13, 2005).
This informative article from National Public Radio reports on the environmental effects of the 2004 Indian Ocean tsunami.

BBC News. n.d.
http://news.bbc.co.uk (May 16, 2005).
The BBC News online provides detailed information on Sri Lanka's population, economy, leaders, and media. It also includes thorough accounts of the 2004 tsunami's effect on Sri Lanka.

Campbell, Verity, and Christine Niven. *Sri Lanka.* Oakland: Lonely Planet Publications, 2001.
This comprehensive travel guide includes information about Sri Lanka's history, politics, culture, food, and landscape, as well as its notable sights and attractions.

Central Intelligence Agency. *The World Factbook: Sri Lanka.* 2005.
http://www.cia.gov/cia/publications/factbook/geos/ce.html (May 12, 2005).
This site presents an overview of Sri Lanka's geography, people, government, economy, communications, transportation, and transnational issues.

Economist.com. 2005.
http://www.economist.com (May 13, 2005).
This site includes a useful fact sheet on Sri Lanka, as well as extensive updates on current events in the country.

The Europa World Year Book 2004. London: Europa Publications, 2004.
This publication provides comprehensive coverage of the recent political events, governments, and economies in countries around the world.

"First Environmental Survey of Tsunami Damage Shows Sri Lankan Coasts and Forests Hurt but Rebounding." *The Nature Conservancy.* February 24, 2005.
http://www.nature.org/pressroom/press/press1797.html (May 13, 2005).
This article summarizes The Nature Conservancy's findings regarding the condition of Sri Lanka's coasts and waters after the 2004 tsunami.

Internally Displaced People: A Global Survey. London: Earthscan Publications Ltd., 2002.
This publication from the Global IDP Project provides information on internally displaced populations. It also includes a regional overview of Asia and the Pacific and a country profile of Sri Lanka.

The International Year Book and Statesmen's Who's Who, 2004. West Sussex, UK, 2003.
This reference book presents detailed data and summaries on the countries of the world, as well as biographies of important international figures.

Library of Congress, Federal Research Division. *Sri Lanka: A Country Study.* 2005.
http://lcweb2.loc.gov/frd/cs/lktoc.html (May 26, 2005)
The Library of Congress describes and analyzes the politics, economy, and culture of Sri Lanka.

Lonely Planet, *Tsunami Update: Sri Lanka.* June 8, 2005.
http://www.lonelyplanet.com/tsunami/srilanka.cfm (June 8, 2005).
The online edition of the Lonely Planet travel guide includes detailed and informative reports on the condition of Sri Lanka after the 2004 tsunami.

Pratap, Anita. *Island of Blood: Frontline Reports from Sri Lanka, Afghanistan, and Other South Asian Flashpoints.* **New York: Penguin Books, 2001.**
This book by journalist Anita Pratap offers firsthand accounts of political violence in several southern Asian countries.

"PRB World Population Data Sheet." *Population Reference Bureau (PRB).* **2004.**
http://www.prb.org (May 15, 2005).
This statistics sheet provides data on Sri Lanka's population, including the infant mortality rate, life expectancy, literacy rate, and other useful information.

Stoffs, Hannah. **"Tsunami's Effects on Agriculture."** In "Waves of Devastation," *University of Wisconsin–Eau Claire.* **Spring 2005.**
http://www.uwec.edu/grossmzc/STOFFSH (June 2, 2005).
This article, part of a website prepared by International Environmental Problems and Policy class students, provides information on the 2004 tsunami's effect on Sri Lanka's farmland.

U.S. Department of State. Bureau of South Asian Affairs. February 2005.
http://www.state.gov/r/pa/ei/bgn/5249.htm (June 30, 2005).
This publication presents a comprehensive profile of Sri Lanka from the U.S. Department of State.

The Virtual Library of Sri Lanka. **2005.**
http://www.lankalibrary.com (May 13, 2005).
This site includes numerous links to informative newspaper articles and books related to Sri Lanka.

Wanasundera, Nanda P. *Sri Lanka.* **New York: Marshall Cavendish, 1996.**
This title is a rich source of information on Sri Lanka's history, economy, government, culture, and more.

"World Urbanization Prospects: The 2003 Revision Population Database." *United Nations.* **2003.**
http://esa.un.org/unup/p2k0data.asp (May 23, 2005).
This statistics sheet provides data and speculations on Sri Lanka's population from the years 1950 to 2030. It includes information on the total population of Sri Lanka, as well as the populations of the capital city and other urban areas.

Bullis, Douglas, and Wendy Hutton. *The Food of Sri Lanka: Authentic Recipes from the Isle of Gems.* **Boston: Periplus Editions, 2001.**
This cookbook features a wide variety of recipes from Sri Lanka, including traditional favorites such as string hoppers and coconut toffee.

Guruswamy, Krishnan. *Sri Lanka.* **Milwaukee: Gareth Stevens Publishing, 2002.**
This title explores Sri Lanka's geography, history, government, art, and recreation.

Katz, Samuel M. *At Any Cost: National Liberation Terrorism.* **Minneapolis: Lerner Publications Company, 2004.**
In this book, terrorism expert Samuel M. Katz examines terrorism and counterterrorism in relation to the Tamil Tigers of Sri Lanka, the Irish Republican Army of Northern Ireland, the ETA of Spain and France, and the Kurdistan Workers Party of Turkey.

Kilgallon, Connor, and Robert Lee Humphrey. *India and Sri Lanka.* **Broomall, PA: Mason Crest Publishers, 2002.**
This book explores the cultural significance and history of traditional costumes worn throughout India and Sri Lanka.

Martin, Rafe. *The Hungry Tigress: Buddhist Myths, Legends, and Jataka Tales.* **Somerville, MA: Yellow Moon Press, 1999.**
This collection of Buddhist writings includes stories about the Buddha as well as tales that highlight key Buddhist values such as wisdom, compassion, and respect for life.

Morris, Ann, and Heidi Larson. *Tsunami: Helping Each Other.* **Minneapolis: Millbrook Press, 2005.**
This book offers an account of the tsunami that swept through southern Asia in 2004.

Narayanan, Vasudha. *Hinduism: Origins, Beliefs, Practices, Holy Texts, and Sacred Places.* **New York: Oxford University Press, 2004.**

This detailed introduction to Hinduism examines the religion's divinities, tenets, sacred texts, and culture.

Pal, Pritya. *Asian Art at the Norton Simon Museum Volume 3: Art from Sri Lanka and Southeast Asia.* **New Haven: Yale University Press, 2004.**
This selection, part of a three-volume set, details more than 150 sacred works of art from Sri Lanka and other Asian countries. All of the featured works are on display at the Norton Simon Museum in Pasadena, California.

Parker-Rock, Michelle. *Diwali: The Hindu Festival of Lights, Feasts, and Family.* **Berkeley Heights, NJ: Enslow Publishers, 2004.**
Learn more about the customs and traditions associated with the Hindu Festival of Lights.

Further Reading and Websites

Pragnaratne, Swarna. *Sinhala Phrasebook*. Oakland: Lonely Planet Publications, 2001.
Use this book to learn some common phrases in the Sinhala language, spoken by more than 70 percent of Sri Lanka's population.

Seneviratne, Suharshini. *Exotic Tastes of Sri Lanka*. New York: Hippocrene Books, 2003.
This cookbook highlights a variety of Sinhalese and Tamil recipes, including curries, vegetarian dishes, and sweet treats.

Sri Lanka Web Server
http://www.lanka.net
This website features links to several Sri Lankan newspapers and informational sources. Visit the Sri Lanka Web Server to read the latest news from publications such as the *Sunday Leader*, the *Daily News*, and *Lanka Business Online*.

Stewart, Gail B. *Catastrophe in Southern Asia: The Tsunami of 2004*. San Diego: Lucent Books, 2005.
This book offers an account of the tsunami that swept through southern Asia in 2004.

Thomas, Gavin. *Rough Guide to Sri Lanka*. New York: Rough Guides, 2005.
This travel guide provides an overview of Sri Lanka's history, cities, people, and sights to see. It also includes many pictures of Sri Lanka.

vgsbooks.com
http://www.vgsbooks.com
Visit vgsbooks.com, the home page of the Visual Geography Series®. You can get linked to all sorts of useful online information, including geographical, historical, demographic, cultural, and economic websites. The vgsbooks.com site is a great resource for late-breaking news and statistics.

Wilkinson, Philip. *Buddhism*. New York: DK Publishing, 2003.
This book introduces readers to the history, practices, and beliefs of Buddhism through detailed text and full-color photographs.

Zimmermann, Robert. *Sri Lanka*. Chicago: Children's Press, 1992.
This book offers a thorough and engaging discussion of various aspects of Sri Lanka, including its history, geography, cities, and culture.

Zwier, Lawrence J. *Sri Lanka: War-Torn Island*. Minneapolis: Lerner Publications Company, 1998.
This title offers a thorough examination of the causes and history of the conflict between Sri Lanka's Tamil and Sinhalese ethnic groups.

Captions for photos appearing on cover and chapter openers:

Cover: The beach of Bentota lost many of these inviting palms in the December 2004 tsunami. The gigantic waves destroyed most of the community's human-made structures too. Only a Buddhist temple, an Islamic mosque, and one or two houses remained standing after the water receded.

pp. 4–5 A carpenter works on a railing for a stairway in Unawatuna, Sri Lanka. Sri Lankans immediately started rebuilding after the tsunami of December 2004 destroyed homes, schools, and businesses.

pp. 8–9 Sri Lanka's coastline is approximately 1,007 miles (1,620 km) in circumference.

pp. 40–41 Workers pick tea by hand at a tea plantation outside of Unawatuna. Most tea is harvested this way. Available machines cannot distinguish between the high-quality leaves at the tips of branches and the coarser leaves nearest the trunk of the plant.

pp. 48–49 Carved into a granite outcropping at the Gal Vihara Temple in Polonnaruwa, Sri Lanka, this colossal reclining Buddha is 46 feet (14 m) long. It dates back to the twelfth or thirteenth century.

pp. 58–59 The tsunami wrecked a tourist restaurant in Kataluwa on Sri Lanka's southern coast.

Photo Acknowledgments

The images in this book are used with the permission of: © Cory Langley, pp. 4–5, 12, 13, 14, 25, 39, 40–41, 48–49, 53, 55, 62; © XNR Productions, pp. 6, 10; © Michael Good/Art Directors, pp. 8–9, 43, 64; © Barbara Swanson/Art Directors, p. 15; © Tibor Bognar/Art Directors, p. 18; © A. A. M. Van der Heyden/Independent Picture Service, pp. 22, 23, 35; © age fotostock/ SuperStock, p. 28; Library of Congress, p. 29 (LC-DIG-ggbain-02553); © Michael Maslan Historic Photographs/CORBIS, p. 30; National Archives, p. 31 (W&C 0954); © Bettmann/CORBIS, p. 33; © ANURUDDHA LOKUHA-PUARACHCHI/Reuters/CORBIS, p. 36; © Joan Wakelin/Art Directors p. 44; AP/Wide World Photos, p. 47; © Ruthi Soudak, pp. 50, 52; © Richard Hammerton/Art Directors, p. 51; © YVES HERMAN/Reuters/CORBIS, pp. 58–59; © Fernando Moleres/Panos Pictures, pp. 61; © Chris Stowers/Panos Pictures, p. 63; Audrius Tomonis-www.banknotes.com, p. 68.

Front cover: © age fotostock/SuperStock. Back cover: NASA